Travel Writing For Fun & Profit: How To Add Dollars To Your Income Writing Travel Articles And Getting Them Published

By Ruth Wucherer

Published by
R & E Publishers
P. O. Box 2008
Saratoga, California 95070

Library of Congress Card Catalog Number
83-62308

I.S.B.N
0-88247-715-3

This book is dedicated

to writers

and would be writers

of travel articles

Table of Contents

INTRODUCTION VII

CHAPTER I   TRAVEL ARTICLE MARKETS
               A THROUGH F 1

CHAPTER II   TRAVEL ARTICLE MARKETS
               G THROUGH O 9

CHAPTER III   TRAVEL ARTICLE MARKETS
               P THROUGH Z. 17

CHAPTER IV   THE TRAVEL WRITER'S
               VOCABULARY 25

CHAPTER V   COMING UP WITH AN IDEA FOR
               A TRAVEL ARTICLE 33

CHAPTER VI   INTERVIEWING TECHNIQUES 39

CHAPTER VII   THE IMPORTANT QUERY LETTER . .43

CHAPTER VIII   WRITING THE ARTICLE 47

CHAPTER IX   TYPING AND MAILING YOUR
               TRAVEL ARTICLE --
               FINAL CHECKLIST. 55

CHAPTER X   PAYMENT FOR ARTICLES, KEEPING
               TRACK OF SALES AND EXPENSES 63

CHAPTER XI   PHOTOS WILL HELP TO SELL
               YOUR ARTICLE 67

CHAPTER XII   ADDRESSES OF STATE TOURIST
               OFFICES 77

CHAPTER XIII   ADDRESSES OF STATE CHAMBERS
                OF COMMERCE. 87

CHAPTER XIV   TEACHING A TRAVEL WRITING
                WORKSHOP/CLASS. 97

CHAPTER XV   REFERENCE MATERIALS FOR
                TRAVEL ARTICLE WRITERS 103

ABOUT THE AUTHOR 107

Introduction

Travel Writing For Fun and Profit is a book writers and would be writers should read. Perhaps you like to travel and would like to learn how to write a travel article – this book will help you. Or maybe you are already a writer and have never thought about writing travel articles – this book will provide valuable instruction.

The first three chapters contain updated information on markets that are currently buying travel articles. Types of articles and photographs needed, pay rates, how to prepare the article, who to send your query letter or manuscript to, and word length are some of the things mentioned in the descriptions.

The book provides you with step-by-step information on how to complete a travel article. Some of the chapter headings are: Coming Up With An Idea For A Travel Article, The Travel Writer's Vocabulary, The Important Query Letter, and Writing The Article, to name just a few.

If you follow the advice in this book, you are bound to make some sales and add dollars to your income. Happy travel article writing!

I Travel Article Markets A Through F

This chapter and the next two contain 30 golden opportunities for you to sell your freelance travel articles. The markets consist of inflight publications (those of the airlines), travel magazines, automobile and travel club publications, recreational vehicle and camping magazines. I have written each publication individually requesting the writer's and photographer's guidelines. The information in these chapters is condensed from the guidelines received. It is very recent and if you follow the specific publication's guidelines, you are bound to make a sale.

Sometimes the writer's and photographer's guidelines are combined. Other times they are separate. In order that you have an idea how one looks, I have included, on page 8 of this chapter, the guidelines verbatim for *Ford Times*.

When a writer is considering submitting a manuscript to a publication, he or she should request the writer's and photographer's guidelines. Always include a self-addressed, stamped envelope with your request. You should also request a sample copy of the publication. Sometimes there is a fee, but often the editor will send it for free if you explain that you are a writer and are thinking of submitting an article to the publication.

There are a few things that I should clarify. One is some of the guidelines say that a manuscript is read on speculation. This means that the editor agrees to look at the author's manuscript but does not promise to buy it until he reads is. This means that the editor has not specifically

1

asked for the manuscript. The best procedure would be to query the editor. See Chapter VII of this book on how to query. Some editors want complete manuscripts before they decided to buy an article.

Payment for travel articles is quite good—usually $.10 a word or more. I do not think that one should send an article to a publication that pays less than $.10 per word. I think this is a fair pay rate because much effort is involved in writing a travel article.

The publications I have mentioned in this chapter and the next two are copyrighted. This means that articles are protected from being reproduced, which is assurance to a writer.

The markets in this chapter begin with the letters A through F. There are nine of them.

ALASKAFEST

Alaskafest, the monthly inflight magazine of Alaska Airlines, is published by Seattle Northwest Publishing Corporation at 1932 First Avenue, Suite 503, Seattle, Washington 98101. All articles are read on speculation. First query the editor.

Despite the title, the magazine is not limited to Alaskan material. California and the Pacific Northwest are also stressed. Writers should remember the following: "The composition of the readership varies with the season. The steady customers, 12 months a year, are business travelers. They make up 70 percent of the passengers in the off-season (non-summer months) and 40 percent during June, July and August, when they are outnumbered by vacationers and summer visitors. Most of the regular business travelers reside (70 percent are male) in Alaska and Washington. We work three months ahead of time."

Articles can run from 500 to 3,000 words. Payment ranges from $40 to $300, made within two weeks of publication.

Photographs should be original color transparencies or black and white prints—do not send dupes, color prints,

110 or 126 film. Payment is $40 to $100 for color photographs used inside, and $125 to $200 for the cover photograph.

Writers should request a "Contributors' Guide" for more detailed information on article and photo payments.

ARIZONA HIGHWAYS

Arizona Highways was recently selected by Writer's Digest as one of the top markets for writers. It is a state-owned monthly designed to attract travelers to and through the state. Most of the material is freelance written; and is slanted to an active, scenic and environmentally oriented adult market, ranging in age from 20 to 55 and often beyond.

Travel articles, all Arizona oriented, are needed. Queries containing a lead paragraph or two and a brief outline of the story or finished manuscripts are wanted. Mail queries and manuscripts to: Copy Editor, Arizona Highways Magazine, 2039 W. Lewis Avenue, Phoenix, Arizona 85009.

According to the "Writer's Guide," "Ideas must be original and stories must utilize creative writing techniques and must have a strong Arizona 'people' flavor in first or thrid person. Readers must be able to share in writers' experiences and observations. The writing itself must be fresh, lively and provocative and material must be carefully researched." A list of sources must be submitted with the final manuscript.

Article length of 2,000 to 3,000 words, for which payment of $.10 to $.20 a word, is negotiated on an individual basis. Payment is made on acceptance.

Photo payments are: $25 for 8x10 size black and white prints; $40 to $150 for 4x5 or larger size transparencies, sometimes smaller sizes are acceptable.

CAMINOS DEL AIRE

Caminos Del Aire is the bi-monthly inflight magazine for Mexican Airlines. All of the magazine is freelance, written and printed in both English and Spanish.

Travel and destination articles of interest to Americans and Mexicans are bought. Manuscript length should be 1,000 to 2,000 words. Buys first North American serial rights.

Photos should be included with manuscript; black and white contact sheets and 2¼x2¼ original color transparencies are wanted. On photos, buys one-time rights plus rights for one reprint.

Manuscripts with photos should be sent to: Editor, Caminos Del Aire, Titsch Publishing Inc., 2500 Curtis Street, Suite 300, Denver, Colorado 80217. All manuscripts are submitted on speculation and paid upon publication of the magazine. Payment is $.10 per published word, including photographs (no extra payment for photos).

CHICAGO TRIBUNE TRAVEL SECTION

The *Chicago Tribune Travel Section* is published weekly at 435 N. Michigan Avenue, Chicago, Illinois 60611.

Approximately 400 travel articles were purchased last year. This newspaper needs destination articles — the approach should be in the second and third person. First person, personal experience articles are avoided but on occasion are bought if they are exceptionally well written. Articles should give the reader positive aspects of a place as well as the negative. The reporting should be accurate; the writing clear and concise.

Article length can be from 800 to 1,500 words, for which the pay rates range from $60 to $125 on publication. Submit completed articles to the editor.

Writers should request the "Free Lance Writer" guidelines which explain in detail what the manuscript should contain and how it should be typed, etc.

"While we prefer first time rights, we do not insist upon them. If your article is being submitted elsewhere, we would like to know where in order to avoid overlapping circulation."

Photos will make your article more saleable. Pay rates for photos are as follows: $5 for PR photos submitted and used, $10-$20 for original black and whites and $60 for each original transparency used on page one.

CONNECTICUT MOTORIST

Connecticut Motorist is a bi-monthly magazine published for members of the Connecticut Motor Club (AAA).

Circulation is 154,000.

Articles are needed on travel and tourist attractions in Connecticut, New England and around the world. They should stress out-of-the-way places, events and activities which are not already familiar to most travelers; and the familiar places, if shown in a new light. Stories should include plenty of accurate documentation; names of hotels and shops, prices paid for lodging, meals, merchandise; with plenty of direct quotes or dialogue of the people who are a part of the story. Article length of 750 to 2,000 words, for which payment rates vary from $75 to $300. Pays on acceptance. Buys all rights. Complete manuscripts preferred.

Good photographs, color or black and white, are essential. One-time rights on photos are purchased with manuscript. Color photo used on front cover pays $50. For photo essays on a single subject, a series of photos (color or black and white), suitable for use with or without an accompanying manuscript, will be considered. Payment is $15 and up per photo.

Send materials to: Director of Publications, Connecticut Motorist, 2276 Whitney Avenue, Hamden, Connecticut 06518.

DISCOVERY

Discovery is the official quarterly publication of the Allstate Motor Club. It has a national circulation of more than one million.

Unsolicited manuscripts are seldom accepted and cannot be returned unless a self-addressed, stamped envelope is provided.

Articles are assigned on the basis of query letters. Query the Editor, Allstate Motor Club, Allstate Plaza, F3, Northbrook, Illinois 60062.

Discovery usually contains one or more major feature articles (2,000-2,500 words) on a regional subject or an area of the country. Shorter articles of 1,000-1,500 words cover seasonal activities, weekend trips and automotive subjects. Buys first North American serial rights. Manuscript rates vary and range from $125 to $750, extra for photos, on acceptance.

Unsolicited photos are seldom accepted and cannot be returned without a self-addressed, stamped envelope. Photography is made on assignment, although resumes and samples are always welcome. Color transparencies (35 mm or larger) are preferred and should show people doing things. *Discovery* pays a day rate plus expenses. All photos are bought for one-time use, with the exception of the cover, which may be used for in-house advertising. Rates will be negotiated.

FAMILY MOTOR COACHING

Family Motor Coaching is the official publication of The Family Motor Coach Association. It is published monthly and 75% freelance written. All manuscripts are looked at on speculation.

Besides travel articles, technical articles are sought that deal with the maintenance and upkeep of motor homes (not trailers or campers). Article length of 1,000-2,000 words. Query first: Managing Editor, Family Motor Coaching, 8291 Clough Pike, Cincinnati, Ohio 45244

Black and white glossy photos preferred or color transparencies. Photos should accompany manuscript but no additional payment is given. Payment for text-photo package ranges from $50 to $200 depending on content and quality. Generally purchases first-time North American rights, exclusive for six months from date of payment.

Writers should keep in mind that the deadline for materials is two months prior to publication date and there is also a thirty day article review period.

FLYING COLORS

Flying Colors is the monthly magazine of Braniff Airlines. Travel pieces must deal with Braniff destinations. It is best to query first—stating the working title of the proposed article, the general theme, approximate length and a description of accompanying visuals. Also a brief author biography and two clips of previously published work should be included. Query Editor, Braniff's Flying Colors, 12955 Biscayne Boulevard, North Miami, Florida 33181.

If the query is acceptable, the writer will be given an assignment. The editor will send a memorandum explaining the specifics such as the concept, compensation, deadlines, etc., with respect to the article.

No first person articles will be accepted. The "Editorial Guidelines" state that "Contributors must be absolutely certain that all material provided is accurate and up to date. Facts, figures, people and places should be verified before submission. Substantiation may be required occasionally."

Payment is on publication at a basic rate of $150 per 1,000 words, although variables can and often do affect rates. Buys first rights only.

Photos are included in the article fee and should accompany the article, for one-time use. If a photo submitted with an article is used for the cover, an additional fee is paid. Color photos are needed: 35 mm slide or transparencies sized 2¼"x2¼" or 4"x5". They should be protected in plastic sleeves and mailed with cardboard backings.

FORD TIMES WRITER'S GUIDELINES

In order that you may see how guidelines look, I have provided, on the following page, a copy of the *Ford Times* Writer's Guidelines.

Ford Times

Published monthly by Ford Motor Company
Room 765, The American Road, Dearborn, MI 48121

Writer's Guidelines

As a magazine for readers who enjoy motoring, *Ford Times* tries, figuratively, to view America through the windshield. That doesn't mean, of course, that all our stories have an automotive connection. Many of our most successful articles have had no link with the automobile; they were published because they interested us. The magazine strives to be lively, informative — and, above all, interesting.

Over the years, we have published original work by a number of celebrated writers. But many of our finest articles have been prepared by writers of no special fame. They succeeded with us — and our readers — because they presented excellent editorial ideas in a highly readable fashion.

Subject matter: Almost anything relating to contemporary American life that is in good taste. Topics include motor travel, vacation ideas, portraits of big cities or small towns, outdoor activities, food, and profiles of interesting people, well-known or otherwise. We have a commitment to originality. We try to avoid stories that have appeared in other publications. However, a fresh point of view and/or superior writing on an old subject will always get our attention. Please note that reports on Ford products and material for the "Famous Restaurants" feature are prepared exclusively by staff members.

Locale: The 50 states, Canada and, to a lesser extent, Mexico and the Caribbean.

Length: A maximum of 1,500 words for full-length stories. Anecdotal items should be limited to one page, double spaced. (Note: Queries are not required for anecdotes.)

Rates: $350 up to $1,000 for full-length stories; $50 for anecdotes. Payment on acceptance.

Submissions: Queries are required. Because of volume, unsolicited manuscripts cannot be reviewed. Please include a self-addressed, stamped envelope.

Illustrations: Speculative submission of high-quality color transparencies *with* manuscripts we have requested is welcomed. We pay $75 for each transparency accepted; a bonus is paid for a cover photo. We want bright, lively, interesting photographs that not only illustrate the text but lend themselves to strong graphic display. Publication releases are required from individuals whose identity is readily apparent in photos. Writers may send snapshots, postcards, brochures, etc., as reference for sketches or paintings. Such artwork normally is done on assignment by the magazine.

The Editors
Ford Times

II Travel Article Markets G Through O

The following travel article markets begin with the letters G through O, actually I through O. The first publication is *Inflight* and the last one is *Off Duty America*.

INFLIGHT

Inflight is Meridian Publishing Company's newest market for freelance writers and photographers. The editor buys 10 to 12 articles and photos for each issue.

The four-color, bi-monthly magazine, produced for commuter airlines for their passengers, features national editorial material in addition to regional articles corresponding to one of seven regions in the country. *Inflight* has a general interest format but predominately male and business-oriented.

Among the articles needed are travel with feature length of 1,200 words or shorter. Writers should keep in mind that work on the magazine is done six months in advance.

Query first with article ideas to: Editor, Inflight, Meridian Publishing Co., Inc., P. O. Box 2315, Ogden, Utah 84404.

Article payment is made on acceptance — $.10 a word. Buys first North American serial rights and second serial (reprint) rights.

As far as photos, good, sharp, pro-quality color and black/white photos are essential. In color, Kodachrome is preferred. Photo payments are $20 for black/white photos and $25 for color. Buys one-time rights.

KANSAS!

Kansas! is a 32 page, four-color magazine published by the Kansas Department of Economic Development to promote the beauty and economy of the state. The magazine is published quarterly in March, June, September and December and every attempt is made to feature seasonal material in each issue.

Most of the articles and photographs are submitted by freelancers. Material from Kansas writers and photographers is preferred but material is also accepted from out-of-state writers and photographers.

All material should be Kansas-oriented and travel articles should deal with places that are open to everyone.

According to the Writers' and Photographers' Guidelines, "First and most important, a story must have the potential for good color photography. Our photos are the highlight of our magazine and we are interested only in stories with good picture possibilities."

Query with article ideas first to: Editor, Kansas!, Kansas Department of Economic Development, 503 Kansas - 6th Floor, Topeka, Kansas 66603.

Articles should be about 5 to 7 pages of double-spaced typewritten material. Photos should be included with article but no additional payment is given. Good, 35 mm color transparencies are needed. No color prints or black and white photographs.

Generally, pay for articles is between $75 and $150. Sometimes photos are purchased alone, for which a payment of $25 is usually made. Buys first rights to articles and photographs.

LEISUREGUIDE

Leisureguide is a network of city guidebooks distributed in all rooms of major hotels in the following markets: Boston, Florida, Gold Coast (Miami to Palm Beach), Central Florida, Houston, Louisville, South Carolina's Grand Strand (Myrtle Beach and vicinity), Puerto Rico, Chicago, Minneapolis-St. Paul, Milwaukee and Kansas City. The hardcover guidebooks of 86 to 200 pages are updated annually.

Besides the materials the in-house staff prepares, each edition contains a major feature on the particular city, plus shorter features of special interest. These are freelance written. Queries are encouraged so *Leisureguide* editors may advise on topic suitability and editorial approach. All manuscripts are read on speculation; rarely are unsolicited manuscripts purchased.

Send queries and request the "Guide to Editorial Requirements" which lists the manuscript deadlines for the various books to: Editor, Leisureguide, 29901 Agoura Road, Agoura, California 91301.

Payment for major articles of 1,500 to 2,000 words is $300. For shorter features (250 to 750 words), payment ranges from $50 to $125. Buys full rights. Photos purchased without manuscript or on assignment. Payment rates are negotiated with the photographer.

MICHIGAN LIVING/AAA MOTOR NEWS

Michigan Living/AAA Motor News is a monthly magazine published by the Automobile Club of Michigan for its one million members. Queries are welcome but a decision is not made to buy unless a writer submits a completed manuscript. Travel pieces, special events, camping, winter sports and outdoor activities (all stressing Michigan) are needed.

The "Guide for Freelance Material" says, "Our readers want articles that verbally and colorfully transport them to the areas described, yet avoid travel writing cliches such as 'Paradise for sightseers' or 'Mecca for camera fans.' Travel attractions should be appraised honestly and objectively, stressing both good and bad points. In addition to describing things to see and do, articles should contain accurate, current information on costs the traveler would incur. On the strength of the article alone, readers should be able to decide whether or not they would enjoy visiting the area in the future, by the sounds, sights, tastes and smells described.

Most articles are 1,000 to 1,500 words for which the author is paid $175 to $300 on acceptance. For shorter articles of 500 to 800 words, authors are paid $100 to $150 on acceptance. Copies of the magazine are sent to the author when his or her article appears.

Black and white photos are included in the article payment. Payment for color transparencies is as follows: $150 for a cover photo and $25 to $50 per inside color shot, depending on quality, quantity and size used. Buys first North American serial rights.

Michigan Living publishes several special travel issues a year—Florida and other warm areas in December; Canada (particularly eastern areas) in May; and Michigan in the summer months.

Send articles and queries to: Editor, Michigan Living/ AAA Motor News, Auto Club Drive, Dearborn, Michigan 48126.

THE MIDWEST MOTORIST

The Midwest Motorist is published bi-monthly by the Automobile Club of Missouri for its members. Circulation is 320,000 in Missouri, southern Illinois and Kansas.

Travel articles on areas in the Midwest, as well as the rest of the United States and Europe, are needed.

The editors are looking for "more than the run-of-the-mill travelogue accounts and especially like new twists to old topics." How-to pieces; for example, "How To Travel With Children," are also needed.

The Associate Editor prefers a query letter and copies of a writer's published work, but will also accept complete manuscripts. Send a query letter or manuscript to the Associate Editor at The Midwest Motorist, The Auto Club of Missouri, 12901 North Forty Drive, St. Louis, Missouri 63141.

Articles should be between 700 and 2,000 words in length and pay is between $50 and $200, depending on the length, quality and if the article has already been published elsewhere. Payment is made on acceptance or publication, depending on the situation.

Photos (5x7 or 8x10, black and whites preferred) should be sent with the manuscript. No additional payment is made for photos.

Simultaneous, photocopied and previously published submissions are okay.

MOTORHOME LIFE

Motorhome Life is published nine months a year (except February, October and December). It is devoted to all types of motorhomes, from vans through minis, through large bus-type vehicles, with emphasis on the better living on the road these vehicles can make possible.

Query the editor so he/she can advise on topic suitability and editorial approach; everything is read on speculation. Query Editor, Motorhome Life, Trailer Life Publishing Company, Inc., 29901 Agoura Road, Agoura, California 91301.

Travel features of 1,000 to 2,000 words on trips of specific interest areas are needed. Articles should give detailed information on parks and/or campgrounds where motorhomes can be parked and include maps when possible.

Photos should accompany articles but no additional payment is given. Glossy black and white photos (8x10 size and other sizes) and color transparencies (Kodachrome II - 35 mm and Ektachrome X - 2¼x2¼) are preferred. Photos should depict action as much as possible.

Payment is on publication, up to $175. Buys full rights.

NATIONAL GEOGRAPHIC MAGAZINE

National Geographic Magazine is the monthly magazine of the National Geographic Society which is a nonprofit, scientific and educational organization for increasing and diffusing geographic knowledge and promoting research and exploration. The magazine reaches over ten million homes each month.

Writers should send queries to: Senior Assistant Editor, National Geographic Magazine, 17th and M Streets, NW, Washington, DC 20036.

The magazine especially wants United States regional stories (first-person narratives) with a length varying from 2,000 to 8,000 words. Shorter articles of 2,000 to 4,000 words are particularly needed. Pays on acceptance from $3,000 to $8,000, occasionally more, according to importance of subject, time in field and status of writer.

Buys first publication rights for magazine, with warranty to use the material in other National Geographic

Society copyrighted publications for additional compensation.

Writers need not worry about illustrating their articles because *National Geographic* uses professional photographers. Sometimes, photos are published alone without an accompanying manuscript. Photographers are urged to submit photos on a single subject rather than on many different subjects. Color transparencies only are used: 35 mm are preferred but 2¼x2¼ and larger sizes are acceptable. An initial selection of not more than 50 transparencies is preferred. Payment is based on a space rate of $300 per color page. A minimum of $100 is paid for single transparencies. If you have any questions about submitting photos, please write the Senior Assistant Editor at the same address.

NORTHEAST OUTDOORS

Northeast Outdoors is a monthly newspaper covering camping and outdoor activities in the Northeastern states.

Primary emphasis is on camping since the majority of readers own and use recreational vehicles. The "first person" approach, relating the author's own experiences, is preferred.

Queries are not required, but are helpful for planning and to avoid duplication of subject matter.

Completed articles of five to ten, double-spaced, typed pages are needed. Good black and white photographs, usually of camping scenes, are preferred. Photo sizes can be 3x5, 8x10, or larger; color photos are not acceptable. Send materials to Editor, Northeast Outdoors, 70 Edwin Avenue, P. O. Box 2180, Waterbury, Connecticut 06722.

Payment is upon publication and ranges for $30 to $40 for features without photos or illustrations and up to $80 for features with photographs. Buys all rights.

OFF DUTY AMERICA

Off Duty America is a monthly magazine geared to the off duty military person or family stationed inside the continental United States. Writers should aim their articles toward the age group 20 to 30. Query the U. S. Editor, 3303 Harbor Boulevard, Suite C-2, Costa Mesa, California 92626.

The American edition can only carry one travel story per month, therefore, it has to be broad in scope. An event-related story that can be localized with "where-to-find-it" sidebars is best.

Immediate article needs are for those dealing with big city weekends, state fairs and cruises. Word length should be 1,000 to 1,600 words or shorter.

The Editorial Guidelines stipulate, "We like vivid anecdotes and up-to-date, breezy prose styles. Historical perspectives can easily be overdone. We dislike too many subjective, negative comments about places and peoples. Writers should keep in mind that often our readers are stationed in one place for two or three years. They want and deserve more than a writer's dashed off, first impressions of a place."

Article payment is $.10 per word on acceptance ($.13 for material useful in their overseas editions as well — there are also European and Pacific editions). Buys first serial or second serial rights.

Photo payment is as follows: $25 for black and white, $50 for color, $100 for full page color and $200 for covers.

III Travel Article Markets P Through Z

Here are another 12 markets that need travel articles. If you follow the writer's/photographer's guidelines, you are bound to make a sale.

PACE

Pace, bi-monthly inflight magazine of Piedmont Airlines is in the market for travel pieces (no more than 2,000 words in length) on domestic travels. Articles must deal with destination points of Piedmont Airlines.

A completed manuscript is preferred but query letters can also be sent to: Managing Editor, Pace, Pace Publications, 338 North Elm Street, Greensboro, North Carolina 27401 Payment is worked out between the writer and editor.

PAN AM CLIPPER

Pan Am Clipper is the monthly in-flight magazine for passengers of Pan Am Airlines. The *Clipper* is not necessarily for a United States citizen—perhaps one-third to two-fifths of Pan Am passengers are from countries other than the United States—and there are more than one million of them. Travel articles should deal with Pan Am destinations.

Unsolicited manuscripts will not be read. The best policy is to query the editor with an idea and clips of previously published work. Query Editor, Pan Am Clipper, Ziff-Davis Publishing Co., One Park Avenue, New York, New

York 10016.

If the query is acceptable, the article should be no longer than 1,500 words. Buys first world serial rights. Pay $700 minimum.

Unsolicited photos are not acceptable. Query Photo Editor at the same address. Reviews 8x10 size black and white glossy prints and 35 mm or larger color transparencies. Pays $200/page rate, $400/full page; captions and model releases required, buys one-time rights.

PASSAGES

Passages is the monthly in-flight magazine of Northwest Orient Airlines. Query letters are a must and should be addressed to Editor, 1999 Shepard Road, St. Paul, Minnesota 55116. All articles are on speculation and should stress some aspect of a Northwest route city (writers should obtain a copy of the "Editorial Requirements" for what cities Northwest Orient Airlines goes to).

Travel articles must have a specific story angle. General descriptive pieces about a city or area stressing where-to-shop, where-to-eat and what-to-see should be avoided. Flight-oriented articles should also be avoided. First-person approach is generally acceptable. Article length ranges between 1,000 and 2,000 words. Payment is on acceptance, $100-$150 per article.

Prefers to buy the manuscript and photos as a "package" but sometimes photos may be purchased separately. Highest quality photos, 35 mm and larger are required. Payment for photos is on acceptance. For stock photos, rates range from $50 to $100 for inside color, and from $25 to $75 for black and white, and $200 for covers.

Passages purchases all rights to material used in the magazine, but sometimes will reassign rights to the author after publication, if the author so requests before sale of the manuscript.

SMALL WORLD

Small World is the magazine for Volkswagen owners in the United States and all articles must have a VW tie-in. The magazine is published five times a year.

Articles seldom exceed 1,500 words in length, shorter pieces (around 500 words) often receive closer attention. All work is on speculation; that is, material is examined before a decision is made to purchase or not purchase it. A query is best. Write Editor, Small World, Volkswagen of America, Inc., Englewood Cliffs, New Jersey 07632.

The magazine publishes a variety of articles, including travel. Writers should use a specific, not general, slant when composing a travel article. For example, have an article revolve around a particular person or interest. A good example is "Ghost Towns" (Summer, 1976), an article which explored ruins. The writer traveled in a VW.

Good quality color transparencies (35 mm or larger) are a must. Signed model releases are required from all individuals appearing in photographs to be used in *Small World*.

Payment for feature article (text and photographs) is $100 per printed page, on acceptance. Buys all rights.

TRAILER LIFE

Trailer Life is a monthly magazine which informs all RV enthusiasts, regardless of the type of vehicle they own. Personal experience articles must be very interesting; merely living in or traveling by trailer is not enough. Articles should give detailed information on parks and/or campgrounds where trailers can be parked and include maps when possible. Shorter pieces of 100-250 words on interesting places off the established routes, with a couple of photos, are also needed.

Query first: Editorial Director, Trailer Life, TL Enterprises, Inc., 29901 Agoura Road, Agoura, California 90301. Everything is read on speculation.

Photos should accompany article but no additional payment is given. Glossy black and white photos (8x10 size and other sizes) and color transparencies (Kodachrome II - 35 mm and Ektachrome X - 2¼x2¼) are preferred. Photos should show action and be as close up as the subject matter will allow.

Payment is on publication, up to $175. Buys full rights.

TRAVEL & LEISURE
Travel & Leisure is a monthly magazine. Assignments are only made on the basis of query letters, which should be directed to Vice President/Managing Editor, 1350 Avenue of the Americas, New York, New York 10019.

Writers should study the magazine closely before submitting queries. Best place to break in is one of the regional sections—New York Metro (NYM), Eastern (E), Chicago Metro (CM), Midwestern (MW), California (C), Far Western (W) or Southern (S). Articles published in these regional sections pay $600. Large feature articles may pay up to $2,000.

All payment is on acceptance. Buys first North American serial rights.

Photo assignments are made mainly to established photographers. *Travel & Leisure* pays expenses.

UNITED MAINLINER
United Mainliner is the monthly in-flight magazine of United Airlines. Travel pieces that relate to United's route map are needed. Query first in one page or less to: Editor, United Mainliner, East/West Network, Inc., 34 East 51st Street, New York, New York 10022.

Article length should be 1,500 to 2,000 words. Payment is from $250 to $700. Wants no photos to be sent by writers.

USAIR MAGAZINE
USAir Magazine is a monthly general interest magazine published for airline passengers, many of whom are business travelers. The magazine publishes a variety of articles including travel (traditional destinations and off-beat places).

Articles range in length from approximately 750 to 2,500 words. Payment is between $250 and $750 on acceptance. Buys first rights. Query first: Editor, USAir Magazine, Ziff-Davis, 1 Park Avenue, New York, New York 10016.

Since the magazine wants to be as visually appealing as possible, special attention is given to those articles that can be strikingly illustrated with photographs or original artwork. Minimum payment for photos is $75. Full-page rates are $150 for black and white, and $200 for color. Occasionally, photographic assignments are given, for which payment of $250 per day is made. Buys one-time rights on photos.

VISTA/USA

Vista/USA is the magazine of Exxon Travel Club. It is published quarterly, with special issues published from time to time, and distributed to about one million club members throughout most of the United States. Since the magazine has about 30 editorial pages per issue, it is very selective with its article choices. Writers should keep in mind that the magazine works 15 to 18 months ahead of time.

Queries or finished manuscripts are acceptable. Feature articles on North America, Hawaii, Mexico and the Caribbean that appeal to a national audience are needed. Length is usually about 2,000 words and payment starts at $500, payable on acceptance. Rates for shorter features vary according to length.

According to the "Writer's Guidelines," "Articles should have definite themes and should give our readers an insight into the character and flavor of an area. . . .Good use of anecdotes and quotes should be included. Above all, do not submit articles about an automobile trip you have taken from one point to another."

Also 500-word articles are bought for the Places of Interest column. These are North American or other places that do not warrant feature-length coverage, yet are unusual and interesting. Payment is $125 per item.

Buys first North American serial rights on all articles.

If you decide to query, emphasize something about the approach you would take in writing about an area. One-page outlines are preferred but not necessary. Please do not cover more than one idea per paragraph. Finished manuscripts or queries should be sent to Editor, Vista/USA, Box 161, Convent Station, New Jersey 07961.

As far as photos, unsolicited ones will not be considered. Interested photographers should submit a detailed, up-to-date list of the subjects they cover. Photos must be in color and must be accompanied by complete photo identification as to where and when the pictures were taken as well as have your name on them. Rates for one-time use of color transparencies (any size) are as follows: $135 for 1/4 page, $150 for 1/2 page, $175 for 3/4 page, and $200 for full pages; Places of Interest $100; front cover $350; and back cover $300.

WESTERN'S WORLD

Western's World is the bi-monthly inflight magazine of Western Airlines. Most of the articles and editorial features appearing in the magazine are the work of established writers, working on assignment. Very little unsolicited material is published but query letters and suggestions are welcome for future pieces. Address queries to Editor/Publisher, 141 El Camino Drive, Suite 110, Beverly Hills, California 90212.

Preferred length of manuscripts is 1,200 to 2,000 words. Payment is made on publication at the rate of $.10 per word. Buys all rights.

Photos of the area served by Western Airlines are welcome: Alaska to Mexico, Hawaii to Minneapolis/St. Paul, and all points inclusive. Transparencies of 2¼" or larger and 35 mm slides are preferred. Very little black and white work is published. Photo payment is on publication and ranges from $25 to $100 for inside use. For covers, payment is higher and subject to negotiation. Photos are bought at one-time rights only and photographers are free to sell their work again.

WOODALL'S CAMPING HOTLINE

Woodall's Camping Hotline is a monthly magazine geared to older couples and families with older children who want useful information on their favorite pastime—camping and traveling throughout North America in recreation vehicles.

Travel articles should be slanted to vacation trips and areas that RV owners would like to see. According to the "Guidelines For Writers," the writing style should be "enthusiastic, light, enjoyable and easy to read and understand—definitely not verbose—concise without being cryptic."

Article lengths should be 1,000 to 2,000 words.

Black and white or color photos are purchased with manuscript; no additional payment is made. Payment is about $.10 a word on acceptance. Buys all rights, but will reassign them to author after publication.

Query or submit complete manuscript to Editor, Woodall's Camping Hotline, 500 Hyacinth Place, Highland Park, Illinois 60035.

WORLD TRAVELING

World Traveling is a bi-monthly magazine published by Midwest News Service, 30943 Club House Lane, Farmington Hills, Michigan 48018. Mail queries to the Editor. About 75% of the magazine's material is freelanced.

Recent articles were published on Korea, Bermuda, Salt Lake City and Australia.

Complete manuscripts are also acceptable and should be around 1,000 words. Pays on publication $100 for 1,000 words, buys all rights.

Black and white photos or color transparencies should accompany article. Pays $10 for black and white photos, $10 for color transparencies; buys one-time rights on photos.

IV The Travel Writer's Vocabulary

Here is a vocabulary of 75 terms that the travel writer should be familiar with. Many are writing and printing terms while others specifically refer to travel. They are listed alphabetically.

All rights – Under this term, a writer forfeits the right to use his or her material in its present form elsewhere. Some magazines require this either because of the top prices they pay for material or the fact that they have book publishing interests or foreign magazine connections.

Assignment – An editor asks a writer to do a specific article for which he or she usually names a price for the completed manuscript.

Bi-monthly – A publication that is published every two months.

Bi-weekly – A publication that comes out every two weeks.

Bold face – The dark form of a type family as compared to its medium and light forms. Usually chapter headings and subheadings are set in this so that they stand out.

Byline – The writer's name is put on the article, usually at the top but sometimes at the end of the article. Most writers usually receive a byline plus payment for their work.

Circ. — Abbreviation for circulation. For example, the *1984 Writer's Market* states that *National Geographic Magazine* has a circulation of 10,700,000.

Clips — If an editor is working with you for the first time, sometimes he or she requests clips of your previously published work.

Column inch — All the type contained in one inch of a typeset column.

Complete manuscript — Some editors prefer the entire written article rather than a query.

Composition — Typesetting which can be done by machine or hand.

Contributor's copies — Copies of the issue of a magazine sent to an author in which his or her work appears.

Copy — Manuscript material before it is set in type.

Copy editing — Editing the manuscript for grammar, punctuation and printing style as opposed to subject content.

Copyright — Usually most publications are copyrighted, meaning that the authors' works are protected from reproduction.

Correspondent — A writer away from the home office of a newspaper or magazine who regularly provides it with copy.

Cover letter — This is a letter that is submitted with your completed manuscript. It should summarize your article and also remind the editor that you agreed to work on it.

Dateline — The date and place of writing an article. This is put in bold face at the start of the first paragraph of the article; for example, Washington, DC (followed by the body of the article). The date is on the top of the page of the newspaper or magazine so it is not repeated here.

Destination — Inflight magazines (published by airlines) frequently use articles about places where final landings are made.

Domestic — Refers to travel in the United States, as opposed to foreign travel.

Feature article length — A lead article in the magazine. Usually it is longer.

First rights only — The writer offers the magazine the right to publish the article the first time. Also referred to as first serial rights and first North American serial rights.

Free sample copy — An editor usually will send a free sample copy if the writer requests one. Sometimes there is a charge.

Freelance writer — A writer who is not under contract for regular work but sells his writings to any buyer. The higher percentage of freelance work a publication buys, the better are the chances for the writer to sell his or her work. Also, many publications buy a lot of freelance work because they have small editorial staffs.

Honorarium — A token payment. It may be a very small amount of money or simply a byline and copies of the publication in which your material appears.

Inflight — Refers to the publications put out by airlines; such as, *Passages* is the monthly inflight magazine of Northwest Orient Airlines. If you have ever flown, often you are told to take the free copy of the airline's inflight magazine that is in your seat.

Justification — The process of spacing out type to a given measure so that lines may be uniform. This is why columns in a magazine and newspaper all have the same width.

Kill fee — The writer is paid a portion of the agreed-on fee for a complete article that was assigned but which was subsequently cancelled.

Layout — The "blueprint" of a magazine that shows where copy, photos and ads go.

Market — Refers to a publication or book publishing company that is currently buying freelance material. For example, the *1984 Writer's Market* lists 4,000 markets which are currently buying material.

Measure — Width of a column of set type. The columns are all equal.

Memorandum — Once an assignment is made, an editor, in some cases, sends a letter to the writer explaining how the article should be developed, compensation, deadlines, etc. This way, both the writer and editor have a clear understanding of each other's obligations.

Monthly — A magazine that comes out every month.

Ms. — Abbreviation for one manuscript.

Mss. — Abbreviation for more than one manuscript.

One-time rights — Buying rights for only one-time. Usually magazines buy photos for one-time rights.

Package sale — The editor buys a manuscript and photos as a "package" and pays the writer with one check.

Page rate — Some magazines pay for material at a fixed rate per published page, rather than so much per word.

Payment on acceptance — The writer is paid when the article is accepted, before it is published.

Payment on publication — The writer is paid after the article is published.

Pen name — The use of a name other than your legal name on articles, stories or books where you wish to remain anonymous. Simply notify your post office and bank that you are using the name so that you'll receive mail and/or checks in that name.

Photo feature — A feature in which the emphasis is on the photographs rather than any accompanying written material.

Photocopied submission — Is acceptable to some editors instead of the author sending the original manuscript.

Photographer's guidelines — Guidelines a writer should follow in sending photos with a manuscript. Sometimes they are separate or included with the writer's guidelines.

Photos — These are almost a must for selling your travel article. Some publications ask writers to submit text-photo packages in which there is no additional payment made for photos. In other cases, there is an additional payment for photos. See the chapter on photos for definitions of such terms as: glossy, color transparency, etc.

Pix — This term is interchangeably used with photographs.

Proof — Impression pulled from a cut or a body of type for examination or correction.

Public domain — Material which was either never copyrighted or whose copyright term has run out.

Quarterly — A publication that comes out every quarter, three months, or four times a year.

Query — A letter to the editor to try to elicit interest in your proposed article. Always include a self-addressed, stamped envelope (SASE) with your query.

Regional publication — A magazine that is devoted to a certain area. The material submitted must pertain only to that area.

Rejection slip — A letter to the writer explaining that the publication cannot use your completed manuscript. Sometimes this is a form letter.

Reporting time — The number of days, weeks, etc., it takes an editor to report back to the author on his or her query or manuscript.

Repro proofs — Proofing on special paper to assure perfect reproduction.

Royalties, standard hardcover book — 10% of the retail price on the first 5,000 copies; 12½% on the next 5,000, and 15% thereafter.

Royalties, standard mass paperback book — 4% to 8% of the retail price on the first 150,000 copies sold.

RV — Abbreviation for a recreational vehicle (motorhome, camper, trailer, etc.). Many publications devoted to recreational vehicles buy travel articles.

SASE — Abbreviation for self-addressed, stamped envelope.

Second serial (reprint) rights — This gives the magazine or newspaper the opportunity to reprint an article after it has already appeared in some other publication.

Semi-monthly — A publication that is published twice a month.

Semi-weekly — A publication that comes out twice a week.

Sidebar — A feature presented as a companion to a straight news report (or main magazine article) giving sidelights or human-interest aspects, (or) sometimes explaining just one aspect of the story.

Simultaneous rights — This term refers to the same article being sold simultaneously to two or more publications which do not have overlapping circulations.

Simultaneous submission — Submitting the same article to several publications at the same time.

Slant — The approach the writer should use in preparing his or her article so that it will appeal to readers of a specific magazine. See writer's guidelines for this information.

Solicited manuscript — One that is requested by the editor.

Speculation — The editor agrees to look at the author's manuscript but does not promise to buy it until he or she reads it.

Stringer — A writer who submits material to a magazine or newspaper from a specific geographical location.

Style — The way in which something is written; for example, punchy sentences of flowing, narrative description or heavy use of quotes of dialogue.

Submission — The act of submitting a manuscript to an editor.

Tabloid — Newspaper format publication on about half the size of the regular newspaper page.

Tearsheet — Page from a magazine or newspaper which contains your printed article. Usually the editor will send you the entire issue. (See "contributor's copies" in this section.)

Uncopyrighted publication — The publication does not protect the author's work because it is not copyrighted. It is in the public domain and can, therefore, be easily reproduced.

Unsolicited manuscript — An article that an editor did not specifically ask to see.

Writer's guidelines — Writers should follow a publication's guidelines when preparing an article. Often these guidelines will be sent for free if the writer requests them. Sometimes guidelines for submitting photographs are included. At other times, they are separate.

V Coming Up With An Idea For A Travel Article

The information on markets which I have provided has most likely given you some ideas for travel articles.

Let me first state some generalities. You must have a great interest in the subject you plan to write about (otherwise you will not be able to arouse interest in the reader). The subject you choose to write about must be timely. For example, say you want to write about Mount Vernon, George Washington's home — you can write about the history but, in addition, should include information on what is happening today. The idea you want to write about must not be too narrow or broad in scope. In both of these cases, it would be hard to write an article because you would end up with too few or too many words.

The subject you plan to write about should be fresh, not covered recently by the publication. Try to use a different angle when writing your article. Carry a notebook along with you when you travel. In this way, you can easily jot down notes about places you were impressed with, as well as important addresses and facts that may be helpful to you in developing a travel article. Pick up some of the brochures at the tourist sites you are visiting.

When querying an editor, submit several ideas at one time. If the editor does not like one idea, he or she can select another one. This way you will not have to waste time typing up individual query letters.

Now I would like to suggest broad categories which will help you come up with a travel article idea. You do not have to limit yourself to these categories.

- *Museums* — These include general and specialty museums. For example, in Cody, Wyoming, there is a museum devoted to Buffalo Bill. I visited it about three years ago and found it to be very interesting.

- *Amusement Parks* — Examples are Disney World, Disneyland, Great America and Six Flags.

- *Specialty Parks* — These are parks that are devoted to a special interest. For example, at Kentucky Horse Park in Lexington, one can view exciting horse races as well as the horses, horse equipment and the museum.

- *Gardens* — Examples are Cypress and Busch Gardens.

- *Mansions* — In this category, I put people's lovely homes which are open to the public for viewing. Some of them are historical sites. Examples are, House on the Rock near Spring Green, Wisconsin; Hearst Castle in San Simeon, California; George Washington's home in Mount Vernon, Virginia; and the Biltmore House and Gardens in Asheville, North Carolina.

- *Shopping Malls* — New shopping malls in your area could be a subject for a travel article.

- *Wineries* — I think a winery is an excellent idea for a travel article.

- *Zoos* — This is one place you can take your family and the cost is not that much.

- *Natural Wonders* — These would include mountain ranges, waterfalls, forests, deserts, etc. Examples are the Smoky Mountains, Yellowstone National Park and Niagara Falls.

- *Boat Cruises* — A cruise of a specific area can make

an interesting subject for a travel article. For example, when I was in New York, I took a "Circle Line" cruise of Manhattan Island.

- *Raft Trips* — This is another possibility for a travel article. When I was out West three summers ago, I took the mild raft trip down the Snake River in Jackson, Wyoming. This is one that you really enjoy and you do not get that wet.

- *Historic Sites* — These are favorites such as the United Nations, the White House, Statue of Liberty and Jefferson Memorial.

- *An Individual City or Country* — This is the usual subject for a travel article. For example, what is exciting and interesting about Philadelphia, Denver, etc., or what makes France, London or Italy unique?

Above I have mentioned a few categories that would be helpful to you in coming up with an idea for a travel article. Check with your local travel bureau for additional ideas.

MILWAUKEE AND WISCONSIN AS EXAMPLES

Attractions in your own city and state should give you ideas for travel articles. I will take the city in which I live— Milwaukee, Wisconsin—as an example. Just to give you a little background on the city, Milwaukee is the 11th largest city in the United States with a population of about 700,000 (including suburbs).

It is located in southeastern Wisconsin and is primarily industrial. Among its outstanding attractions are:

- *The Mitchell Park Conservatory* where one, for example, can experience the desert and tropical rain forest by going through three flower and plant domes -- 750,000 cubic feet each.

- *The Milwaukee County Zoo* which has 184 acres. It

is especially noted for its petting animal area where children can play with and feed the animals.

- *The Grand Avenue Mall*, a series of retail stores and eating places, which opened in Downtown Milwaukee in August of 1982.

- *The Milwaukee Public Museum* which is one of the half dozen largest and certainly one of the best known museums of natural history in the United States. One of its captivating exhibits is "Streets of Old Milwaukee" which depict Milwaukee life at the turn of the twentieth century.

- *Boerner Botanical Gardens* in the suburban Hales Corners which has a magnificent rose flower collection in the month of June.

- *Summerfest* – An annual event, lasting 11 days and held at Milwaukee's lakefront. Among the things featured are famous singers, musical groups, the circus and rides.

Wisconsin is a beautiful state noted for its natural wonders, especially in the northern part. It has about 4,000,000 people. Here are some of its outstanding attractions:

- *Door County* – Many artists and craftspeople live here year-round or for the summer. Artists capture the beauty of this area in their drawings and paintings. Door County's Peninsula State Park, the largest in the state, is located between Fish Creek and Ephraim. The winding woodland roads through the park are unusually breathtaking.

- *Lake Geneva Cruises* – Board the Walworth II mail boat which delivers mail to lake shore residents. The mailman delivers the mail by actually jumping off the moving boat onto the dock and then leaps back aboard in one swift motion. You can also tour Lake Geneva on two other boats, the "Lady" and "Belle."

- *The House on the Rock* is one of the midwest's top tourist attractions. Near Spring Green, it was built on a massive chimney rock by sculptor Alexander Jordan in the mid 1940s. It has expanded and includes numerous components; such as, the Water Garden, Mill House, Gate House and Streets of Yesterday.

- *Stone Mill Winery* — Want to find out the secrets of how to make good wine? Then visit the Stone Mill Winery in Cedarburg, about 35 miles north of Milwaukee. Here three wines under the "Newberry" label are made — Natural Cherry, Colonial Spice and Honey Cherry.

- *Wisconsin Dells* is one of the state's top attractions featuring the Tommy Bartlett Water Ski Show, the Duck Ride and Indian Ceremonial.

- *Cave of the Mounds* — Interested in how cave formations are made, then visit this exciting attraction near Blue Mound.

- *Madison* — Wisconsin's capitol is a bustling place to visit. You may get an opportunity to meet the governor. Some Milwaukee travel agencies offer a day's tour to the capitol.

- *Old World Wisconsin* — You would enjoy spending the day at this noteworthy attraction in Eagle, Wisconsin. There are more than 40 authentic, original structures representative of the many different ethnic groups who settled in Wisconsin.

- *Baraboo* — This is the home of the Circus World Museum.

I have tried to give you some specific ideas for travel articles. I have visited most of the places mentioned. You probably have similar attractions in the city and state where you live.

VI Interviewing Techniques

When preparing a travel article, you might have the occasion to interview one or several people and incorporate that material in your article.

Say you were staying at a resort. Besides writing about your experience, you might want to interview the manager of the resort. His or her comments would give your article an interesting angle.

HOW TO INTERVIEW

Follow these hints and your interview should be successful:

- Make an appointment with the person you want to interview. Do not just drop in.

- Be on time for the interview.

- Allow enough time for the interview so you and the person will not be rushed.

- Prepare some questions ahead of time so that your interview will proceed smoothly.

- Determine a specific angle ahead of time so your questions will flow in that direction.

- As you go on with the interview, additional questions will be generated.

- If possible, find out some information about the person ahead of time. This way, both of you will feel comfortable at the onset of the interview. It is also a good way to start the interview.

- Use a notebook or tape recorder if the person feels comfortable with that arrangement.

- Look the person directly in the eye when interviewing him or her.

- Ask the person to repeat quotes if you think you do not have them down correctly, or, in fact, repeat any information that you did not completely understand.

- Before you leave, thank the person for taking the time to be interviewed. A follow-up thank you note is suggested.

WRITING UP THE INTERVIEW

I recommend that you look through your local newspaper for interviews. Read them and you will obtain a feel for how an interview should be written.

The following are some helpful suggestions for writing up the interview:

- Use as many direct quotes as possible.

- Include some indirect quotes.

- Vary the writing style—perphaps use a direct quote, factual information and an indirect quote. Intersperse your quotes with your other information to make the article more interesting.

- Instead of always using he/she said—other words that can be used are—commented, explained, suggested, pointed out, noted, elaborated on, added, stated, etc.

- If the quote is several sentences long, you do not always have to put he/she said after each sentence. It is understood that the same person is speaking.

- Sometimes the person interviewed requests that you show them a copy of the final interview before submitting it to the editor. This way he or she will be able to verify if the quotes are accurate. If there is time, let the person see it, though it is not required.

- Write up the interview in the past tense unless the editor requests otherwise.

- After you have written up the article which contains the interview material, it is a good idea to send a copy of it to the person with a note thanking him or her for the time spent on the interview.

- If the article appears in published form, send a copy to the person you interviewed.

VII The Important Query Letter

The query letter is simply a letter asking the editor if he or she would be interested in seeing your manuscript for possible publication. Most travel editors require that you submit a query letter before completing the manuscript. It saves both you and the editor time.

For example, if the editor is not interested in the article and tells you so by replying negatively to your query letter, you either can send the query letter to another editor or forget the idea completely. You probably will want to do the former. On the other hand, if the editor reacts favorably to your letter, he/she is giving you the go ahead to write the article. Still, he/she is not committed to publishing the article unless that was the agreement.

INCOMPLETE QUERY LETTER

Date

Editor's Name
Name of Publication
Address

Dear (Name):
    I would like to submit an article on Mackinac Island for possible publication. Please let me know if you are interested.

                Cordially,
                (Name and address)

What is wrong with the query letter on page 43?
Mainly, the letter is incomplete—it hardly says anything.
What, then, are the elements of a good query letter?

ELEMENTS OF A GOOD QUERY LETTER
Here are eleven elements of a good query letter:

- Address the letter to a specific person, find out the editor's name or the specific person who looks at queries.
- Tell the editor how you found out about the publication. This would make a good introduction.
- Mention the main subject that your manuscript will cover. Add details such as attractions, historical sights, hotels (current rates, if possible), restaurants, shops, admission fees, etc.
- Length of article—should adhere to what publication has stated. State the length you think your article will be.
- The time it will take you to complete the article.
- Availability of photos and types—black/white glossies, color transparencies, etc.
- State if you have had any other articles published. Sometimes this may help you get the assignment.
- Mention if you are submitting this idea to other editors. I think this is okay, though I would never submit the same article to two different editors at the same time. Some authors do but I think the procedure is not good ethics.
- Ask for copies of the writer's and photographer's guidelines and the publication. These will give you additional information on how to prepare your manuscript. Many times, the editor will send these free of charge.
- Type your query letter single-spaced on white paper, preferably about one page. Make a copy for your file.
- Include a stamped, self-addressed, number 10 envelope for a reply. This is one of the cardinal rules of writing. If you do not do this, most editors will not reply. If you do, you should receive a reply with a month or less.

EXAMPLE OF A GOOD QUERY LETTER
The following is an example of a good query letter:

Date

Editor's Name
Name of Publication
Address

Dear (name):
I read in the May issue of THE WRITER magazine that you are interested in receiving travel articles for your publication (name).

I am an avid traveler and would like to submit an article on Mackinac Island in Michigan which I visited last summer. Mackinac Island has many attractions to offer—peacefulness (no automobiles are allowed on the island), numerous historical sights, boat cruises, hotels, restaurants, shops and more. I stayed at the Grand Hotel and would like to include some information on it.

The article would run about 800 words and would take me about three weeks to complete. I will include a couple of black and white glossy photos of the Grand Hotel.

I have a number of travel articles published in such publications as ACCENT, LET'S GO PLACES and GRACIOUS LIVING magazines; THE MILWAUKEE JOURNAL newspaper and others.

If you are interested in having me write an article on Macinac Island, please let me know. Also, send me copies of the writer's and photographer's guidelines and your magazine. I hope to hear from you in the very near future.

Sincerely,
(signature)
Name (typed)
Address (typed)

VIII Writing The Article

The actual process of writing an article usually takes much work. Let us say that an editor reacts favorably to your idea and gives you the go ahead. Here are ten suggestions to help make the writing easier:

1. Adhere closely to the word length that the publication states.
2. Put your article in the third person unless the editor says differently.
3. Keep your article in the same tense throughout unless you definitely have to switch in spots.
4. Think of a short and snappy title that will stimulate the reader to read on.
5. Write a strong lead paragraph that will encourage the reader to read on further.
6. Add details in the middle paragraphs to help keep the article moving—unique attractions, admission fees, hotels with price ranges and location are some of the things that should be included if appropriate.
7. Compose an ending that sums up the article; in other words, do not leave it hanging.
8. Make sure spelling and punctuation are correct. Keep Webster's at your side.
9. Reread the article over several times before mailing it to make sure that it has continuity and says what you wanted to say.
10. Make sure all the information in the article is accurate. Double check admission fees, hotel rates, people's

names if used, etc. This will establish your credibility with the editor.

WRITING APPROACHES

There are many writing approaches you can use. They include: centering it around a person, event, anniversary; historical approach; moving approach—for example, if it is an article on a cruise, make the reader feel like he or she is going on a cruise, etc. Sometimes you can combine a couple of approaches. Think of a fresh angle; this will make your article interesting.

I wrote an article titled, "Hershey, Pennsylvania: Chocolate Capital of the World," which was published in *Accent* magazine a few years ago. The article combines two approaches (centering it around a person and telling about attractions). A major portion of the article is devoted to Milton Hershey, the inventor of the famous chocolate bar. Another portion deals with the attractions at the visitor center and Hershey Park. Two photos, one of Milton Hershey and the other of equipment for chocolate production, added wonderful touches to the article. I might further state that I was paid very well for these glossy black and white photos ($20 a piece) and they were not mine. I obtained them from the Hershey Corporation.

VERBATIM TEXT OF HERSHEY ARTICLE

Following is the verbatim text of the entire article which was relatively short (about 365 words) but with the photos, it filled up one magazine page nicely:

"Hershey is a place where one can enjoy eating and learning about chocolate bars and candy kisses.

The Hershey complex consists of a visitor center, plant and park. It is located eight miles north of the Pennsylvania Turnpike.

Before June 30, 1973, visitors toured the plant to find out the secrets of how the delicious Hershey chocolate products are made. But the plant tour was discontinued and replaced by the visitor center, 'Hershey's Chocolate World.'

In the center, visitors board a free automated ride which conveys them over 1,200 feet of track, past 25 scenes illustrating the story of chocolate—from the growing and harvesting of cocoa beans in the tropics through the basic steps in the production of chocolate at Hershey's famous plant. Children will enjoy Hershey Park, which has numerous rides and an animal contact area. The entrance to the park is Tudor Square, a 17th century English setting with a castle. Milton Snavely Hershey was the man behind the original Hershey products. Born in Derry Township in 1857, he quit school at the age of 15 to become a printer's apprentice. Hershey did not like this type of work and switched to being a candymaker's apprentice. He worked in various parts of the country.

Then he started a caramel business which was unsuccessful at first.

After attending the Chicago Exposition in 1893, Hershey became convinced that caramels were only a 'fad,' and that chocolate would be the basis for a new industry. In 1900, he sold his caramel business and purchased chocolate-manufacturing equipment from Germany.

The chocolate business grew and Hershey decided to move his business from Lancaster to Derry Church, which was renamed Hershey in 1906.

After much experimentation, Hershey developed his own formula for making his original milk chocolate bar. The decision to mass produce this single product, rather than continue with all different chocolate novelties, proved to be a huge success. By 1971, Hershey had $350 million in sales. Visitors can purchase the candy bars and other chocolate confections in 'Hershey's Chocolate World'."

ACCENT MAGAZINE

Accent, a travel-oriented monthly publication with a circulation of 600,000 is 90% freelance written and its main office is in Ogden, Utah. *Accent* is sold to business and industrial firms coast-to-coast who distribute it with appropriate inserts as their "house" magazine. It buys from 120 to 140 manuscripts a year and 200 to 300 photos per year. This market also pays very well—$.10 per word, $20 for black and white photos, $25 for a color transparency and more for color covers.

I was fortunate to have another article published in

Accent titled "Springfield: They Call It." Besides the text, it had a couple of black and white photos—one of the Lincoln Tomb State Memorial and the other of the Lincoln family home on 8th and Jackson Streets (had been their home for 17 years).

I love Springfield, Illinois, because it is so rich in Lincoln history and that is the approach I used in the article. Please take special note of the last paragraph which gives some addresses that may be helpful to the reader. It is one good way to end an article.

VERBATIM TEXT OF SPRINGFIELD ARTICLE

Following is the entire verbatim text of "Springfield: They Call It":

"Springield, Illinois has become know as 'Lincoln Land,' for the life of Abraham Lincoln is reflected everywhere. Lincoln's home, the Old State Capitol and Lincoln's Tomb are some highlights of Springfield.

The Lincoln Home National Historic Site is located on 8th and Jackson Streets. This was the only home the Lincolns ever owned. It was purchased in May of 1844 and Lincoln and his family lived there until 1861 when they departed for Washington. Three of four sons—Edward, William and Thomas—were born in the house. Edward died here on February 1, 1850, at the age of almost four.

The Lincoln home was built in 1839 and is typical of that period. It was a story-and-a-half until 1856 when the Lincolns raised it to two stories. Wooden pegs and handmade nails hold together the native hardwood and white pine.

The Old State Capitol, in the center of downtown, is where Lincoln delivered his famous 'House Divided' speech on June 16, 1858. On May 3 and 4, 1865, his body lay in final state in the Hall of Representatives.

Lincoln's Tomb State Memorial is located in Oake Ridge Cemetery about two and a half miles from downtown Springfield, taking Illinois 97 north.

Lincoln was buried in the original vault on May 4, 1865, but was later moved. A memorial was constructed starting in 1869. The tomb, which was dedicated on October 15, 1874, cost $180,000. It was later reconstructed several times. The remains of Lincoln's wife and three sons are in crypts in the south wall of the chamber.

The eldest son Robert, who served as Secretary of War and Minister to Great Britain, is buried in Arlington National Cemetery.

The large, majestic monument in the center of the burial chamber bearing the simple inscription 'Abraham Lincoln, 1809-1865,' marks the location of the burial vault which is ten feet below the surface of the floor. This marker was taken from the marble quarries of Arkansas and is a solid block of stone. Surrounding the marker are nine flags representing states in which Lincoln and generations of his family lived.

Tourists can see these places by means of bus or walking/driving. The Springfield Mass Transit District offers the Lincoln Shrine One-Hour Tour from June through August. The address is 928 S. Ninth Street, Springfield, Illinois 62703. The Springfield Covention and Tourism Commission offers an excellent brochure on walk/drive tours. The address is: INB Center, Suite C15, 1 N. Old State Capitol Plaza, Springfield, Illinois 62701.''

AN ARTICLE ON NEW YORK

I had a third article published in *Accent* dealing with New York. This article was much longer so I will not provide the entire text but only selected passages. It was enhanced by five black and white photos—one was the Statue of Liberty, a second gave a good look at Manhattan, a third showed the George Washington Bridge, a fourth had the Circle Line Yacht going under the Brooklyn Bridge and a fifth depicted the silhouette of the New York skyline. The article uses the moving approach by giving the reader a feeling that he or she is actually on a cruise seeing the numerous sights.

PASSAGES FROM ARTICLE ON NEW YORK

Here are some selected, verbatim passages from "Take A Cruise—It's The Best Way To See The Big Apple":

"Board the Circle Line Yacht and you're in for a pleasant three-hour, 35-mile cruise around Manhattan Island. Towering buildings, majestic bridges and historic sites await you.

Manhattan, commonly called 'New York,' is only one of the five boroughs which comprise New York City; four of which, including Manhattan, are islands or are part of an island. The other boroughs are: Brooklyn, Long Island, Bronx and Queens.

The Circle Line, measuring approximately 165 feet long, offers comfortable seating for up to 600 passengers. A tour guide provides interesting information about each site.

Starting out at the foot of West 43rd Street (pier 83), Rockefeller Center, Manhattan's financial district, and the Statue of Liberty come into view.

Heading south on the Hudson River, which separates Manhattan from the State of New Jersey, we passed Greenwich Village, which is named for Greenwich, England, and is famous for its poets, writers, artists and actors.

The twin 110-story towers of the World Trade Center dominate lower Manhattan. It houses the United States Customs facilities, offices of many consulates, world trade information service, governmental agencies and private businesses engaged in export-import trade. . . .

Proceed to Upper New York Bay and to your right is Ellis Island, through which 16 million immigrants passed between 1892 and 1954. Abandoned in 1954, the Island was proclaimed as a part of the Statue of Liberty National Monument by President Lyndon Johnson in 1965.

Up ahead is the world's longest suspension bridge, the Verrazano-Narrows, the gateway to the Atlantic Ocean. There are other bridges——the Brooklyn, Manhattan and Williamsburg, which is the largest.

Designed by John Augustus Roebling, the Brooklyn Bridge was twice as long as any in existence in the world at the time. When it was opened on May 14, 1883, a panic developed among the thousands who had come to the ceremonies and 12 people were either crushed to death or killed falling off the bridge.

To the right of the bridge is the borough of Brooklyn, the most populated of the five boroughs, with over three million inhabitants. . . .

The Peter Cooper Village, Empire State Building, United Nations, Queensboro Bridge and Welfare Island come into view. To the right of the Island is Queens, another borough, and to the left on the shore is Gracie Mansion, the home of the New York mayor.

The Circle Line then goes through the East River to Hell Gate, once a dangerous strip of water until the Army blasted the reef. Whirlpool tides still make it a rough spot today. To the right of the East River is Long Island, another borough. The East River leads to the Harlem River. To the right of the Harlem River is the last borough of the Bronx, which is the only borough of New York City located on the mainland of the United States.

As we left the Harlem River, we entered 'Spuyten Duyvil' which joins the Harlem and Hudson Rivers. According to Washington Irving: 'A Dutch trumpeter, one dark stormy night, hurrying with a message from Peter Stuyvesant to the mainland, and no ferryman in sight, vowed to swim across the swirling waters. He cried his boast aloud, shouting that he's cross the turbulent water 'spuyten duyvil'—meaning 'in spite of the devil'.' He did not make it, but his bravery has not been forgotten. . . .

Linking New York and New Jersey is the 14-lane George Washington Bridge. . . .

Other sites include the Chase Manhattan Building, Chrysler Building, Colgate Clock, Yankee Stadium, Woolworth Building and more.

The Circle Line, which has been in operation for over twenty-five years, is a great way to obtain a kaleidoscopic view of Manhattan and the surrounding area. Later one can visit the sites individually. The cruise is given from late March through the middle of November. For information, write: Circle Line, Pier 83, Foot of West 43rd Street, New York, New York 10036."

SUMMARY

The material in this chapter covered several writing approaches that one could possibly use in developing an article. There are other approaches; in fact, invent your own. Strive for uniqueness and interest in your article—that in turn should make the editor want to buy it and the reader want to read it.

If the article is published, do not feel bad if the editor

changes the title or wording of the article and even shortens it. These are usually done because of space requirements.

IX Typing And Mailing Your Travel Article – Final Checklist

I usually do several drafts of my travel article before I do the final draft. I write out the first draft in long hand. I type out succeeding drafts until I feel that the article is perfect.

One thing that you want to accomplish when typing your manuscript is to make it look professional. If you want an editor to even consider your manuscript, make sure that it is neatly typed, that the typewritten copy is not blotted by coffee stains, etc.

It goes without saying that your typewriter should be clean, your ribbon new and so on. Your manuscript should be typewritten and not submitted in long hand. If you do not know how to type, ask or hire someone else to do the job.

Now the job of typing the manuscript begins. Here are ten suggestions to make the task easier:

- Make a carbon copy. This way if the manuscript gets lost, you will have a copy.

- Type your name in the left hand corner of each page.

- Insert the title in capital letters in the center of the first page about a third of the way down.

- Double space your manuscript throughout unless the guidelines have told you differently.

- Use 8½ x 11 size white bond paper.

- Erase errors neatly. I use correction tape. I do not correct the carbon copy. If there are too many errors on one page, I retype it.

- Leave adequate margins of at least 1½" on all four sides. This will give the editor room to write notes in the margin if necessary; for examples, notes to the printer.

- Type each line regularly across the page. You do not have to type your copy into columns; the printer will take care of this.

- On the second page, again type your name in the left hand corner and on the second line, put "Add One" (plus key word of title of article). Do this on successive pages but put "Add Two," "Add Three," etc.

- Put the word "more" on the bottom of each page (centered) until you get to the end of the article where you should put "-0-" (centered).

Pages 57 and 58 are outlines of how the first and succeeding pages should look.

June Fry

Start the article 1/3 of the page down.

LIVE LINCOLN'S LIFE IN SPRINGFIELD, ILLINOIS

1½" margin	body of article double space and indent each paragraph five spaces	1½" margin

more
(Write "more" to indicate that
more follows on next page)

1½" margin

OUTLINE OF SUCCEEDING PAGES OF ARTICLE

June Fry
Add One Lincoln

1½" margin

1½"
margin

continuation of article

1½"
margin

more

1½" margin

Follow the preceding style until you get to the end of your article.

COVER LETTER

Instead of just sending your manuscript to the editor, include a cover letter. This is a good way to remind the editor that you have completed the article and also is an opportunity for you to express your hope that it will be published in the near future. Also state if you are including photos with the manuscript.

The cover letter should be short; no more than one typewritten page. It might read as follows:

Date

Editor's Name
Publication's Name
Address

Dear Editor (name):
Enclosed find an article and three black and white photos on Great America Theme Park, located in Gurnee, Illinois, which is about 55 miles south of Milwaukee, Wisconsin.

About a month ago, I wrote you a query letter saying that I would like to submit an article on this subject. You gave me the go ahead.

I hope that this material is acceptable and that it will be published in the very near future.

Cordially,

Ruth Wucherer
(address)

Enclosures

If you have not heard anything about your travel article within a month, you should inquire about its status.

When you mail your travel article and photos, if you have any, use a manila envelope (10x13 size). Also include another envelope inside, addressed to you and with sufficient postage clipped to it, in case your article is returned.

You can mail your travel article first class or fourth class (the manuscript rate). I always mail my material first class because travel articles are usually not that lengthy and I feel that the article will get there faster.

If you include photos with your manuscript, you should write "Photos Enclosed - Do Not Bend" on the outer envelope. This will alert the mail people that there are photos in the package and hopefully they will handle it with more care and not crush it.

For added protection, you might want to insure your manuscript. Check with your local post office for rates.

I think investing in a miniature postal scale is worthwhile. This way you can weigh your own manuscript and do not have to always make a trip to the post office.

If you have a large manuscript and numerous photos, you may want to put your materials in a jiffy bag rather than a manila envelope. Jiffy bags provide better cushioning. The jiffy bags and postal scale can be purchased at an office supply store or discount store such as K-mart or Target.

TRAVEL ARTICLE CRITIQUE CHECKLIST

Here are 20 points to check yourself on when writing and mailing out your manuscript and photos:

1. Have I requested several copies of the publication I am considering submitting an article to and have I read them thoroughly to get a feel for the style and contents? Often the editor will send the copies for free.

2. Have I queried the editor about my idea unless it says to send the finished manuscript? Have I included a stamped, self-addressed envelope for a reply?

3. The article should be geared towards a specific market. For example, if the publication wants articles on

the Eastern United States, do not send material on the Midwest. Also follow the article length that is specified.

4. Is the subject matter broad enough so an article can be easily written? Still it should not be too broad because then the article would never end.

5. Does the article have a specific angle? For example, it may focus on a certain person, anniversary, attraction, etc. Avoid the familiar.

6. It is best to write the article in the third person unless the writer's guidelines state otherwise.

7. Admission rates, hours open, important addresses, special events, what is unique—are some of the things that should be included in the article.

8. When you travel, carry around a notebook and take down information, collect brochures, etc. This material will be of help when you prepare the article.

9. Remember, if you need photos, you can write directly to the places, state tourist offices or state chambers of commerce. They will often send these photos for free. Be sure that the photos are captioned and properly credited. See the chapters in this book that cover these subjects.

10. Are grammar, punctuation and spellings correct in the article?

11. Type the article on 8½x11 size, white bond paper unless other directions are specified. Reread this chapter for helpful hints on how to prepare a polished manuscript.

12. Are the lead and end paragraphs strong? Does the article flow? Read the article over several times before mailing it out.

13. Have I included an additional stamped, self-addressed envelope in case the article is returned? Is there sufficient postage on the top envelope?

14. Wait about a month for a reply. Otherwise, write the editor to find out the status of your article.

15. On the whole, most publications pay after the article is published. Be patient!

16. You should receive complimentary copies of your article. If you do not, request them.

17. I do not recommend simultaneously submitting the same article to multiple markets. You can easily get into trouble. It is not good ethics.

18. Keep track of your sales as well as expenses; such as, typing paper, ribbons, stamps, etc. You may want to include your writing business on income tax forms. See the next chapter for further information on this subject.

19. If one editor rejects your article, do not get discouraged. Send it to another.

20. Persistence pays off in writing!!!!!

X Payment For Articles, Keeping Track Of Sales And Expenses

After you have written your travel article and submitted it to the editor, you may ask—"When do I receive the check?" It may be awhile because most publications do not pay until the article is published. This may be a few months off. A few publications pay when the article is accepted. A few also offer a kill fee where the writer gets paid a certain fee even if the article is not published.

I would not recommend sending an article to a publication that pays less than $.10 a word. I just do not think it is worth it. Although that is a personal opinion. You can work with lower paying markets in the beginning—then gradually work up to higher paying ones. For example, *National Geographic Magazine* pays $3,000 to $6,000 for articles of 2,000 to 4,000 words. The article has to be excellent as many of you know who read the publication. I believe that this is the highest paying market.

The amount a writer gets paid for an article is usually listed on the writer's and photographer's guidelines. If you have sold several articles to the same editor, you may receive more compensation as time goes on.

One thing that should not discourage a writer is if the editor cuts your original manuscript because of space limitations. This is a common practice. Usually the editor will not tell the writer ahead of time; the writer first finds out when he or she sees the final published article. Sometimes, though, the editor does not cut the article. The editor should send you several copies of the issue in which your work appears. If not, you should request them.

If a writer feels that the article has been substantially changed by the cuts, he or she has a right to complain to the editor. A writer only gets paid for the words that were actually published.

A FEW QUOTES ON PAYMENT

The following are a few quotes on payment to writers. Samuel Johnson, in *Boswell's Life* on April 5, 1776, said this: "No man but a blockhead ever wrote except for money." (Taken from the *Dictionary of Quotations*, collected and arranged and with comments by Bergen Evans, p. 781.)

Mark Twain, in *A General Reply*, said the following about pay: "Write without pay until somebody offers pay. If nobody offers within three years, the candidate may look upon his circumstance with the most implicit confidence as the sign that sawing wood is what he was intended for." (*Dictionary of Quotations*, p. 781) I do not think things will get that bad for most of you travel writers.

Perhaps an editor does not pay you at all for an article. What can you do in this case? First, you could mention it to the editor and hope that he or she will pay you. Second, you could hire a lawyer. But, in most cases, this is not feasible because your payment would not be that high. If you do not succeed in getting paid, I would never work with the editor again.

When you obtain copies of your published article, you should xerox additional copies. I keep copies of all my published works in a scrapbook. For example, when one of my travel articles is published on a certain tourist attraction, I send a copy to the person in charge of the attraction (or the public information officer if it is a large place). They usually write back saying how much they appreciate the publicity.

Occasionally, you receive a small gift in appreciation for writing an article. One time I wrote an article on Mount Vernon, the home of George Washington. I sent a copy to the Mount Vernon Ladies Association, which I mentioned in the story. They, in turn, sent me a beautiful historical book on Mount Vernon.

Also, copies of your published articles are sometimes

requested by editors when you submit a query letter. These published works may help you to get an assignment.

KEEPING TRACK OF SALES AND EXPENSES

If you have sold one travel article in a year, you probably will not want to report in on your yearly federal and state tax forms. It would not be worth all the effort.

On the other hand, let us say that you have had some sales. It is a good idea to get into the practice of keeping track of your sales and expenses. Besides travel article sales, include fees for workshops and speaking engagements (if appropriate). I have done some of the latter. When I record the entries, I put the date I received the check, the title of the article, the publication in which it appeared, and the amount of the check. Here are samples of my entries:

TRAVEL WRITING SALES AND FEES FOR 1982

Date	Title and Name of Publication	Amount
January 15	Hershey, Pennsylvania: Chocolate Capital of the World — Accent	$ 90.00
February 17	Springfield: They Call It — Accent	90.00
March 13	Take A Cruise — It's The Best Way To See The Big Apple — Accent	100.00
April 1	They Kept Mount Vernon From Crumbling To Ruin. . . . — The Milwaukee Journal	50.00
May 1	Gave speech at Wisconsin Regional Writers Association Conference — UW-Marshfield	100.00
May 15	Taught Travel Writing Workshop (3 Sessions) — Sponsored by the Writing Program for Adults, Division of Urban Outreach, University of Wisconsin-Milwaukee and Extension	150.00
	TOTAL	$580.00

Then, after you list all your article sales, speech and workshop fees, if any, calculate the total. This amount should be included as part of your income (gross receipts or sales) on Schedule C (Form 1040) titled "Profit (or Loss) Business or Profession."

Schedule C also has a section for deductions. I will not list all of them but just those that would be associated with a writing business: advertising, car mileage, dues and publications, office supplies and postage, and telephone. You should record these expenses on a regular basis in a notebook or whatever system you choose. When doing your tax return, include these expenses on Schedule C (Form 1040) in the "Deductions" section.

Here is how a sheet that shows your expenses might look:

1982 WRITING BUSINESS EXPENSES

Date	Type of Expense	Amount
January 4	Dues and Publications – 2 year subscriptions to The Writer and Writer's Digest magazines	$40.00
February 10	Supplies and Postage – typing paper and 200 ($.20) stamps	50.00
March 17	Telephone – local business and long distance calls for February	50.00

To arrive at the final amounts, you would have to continually record all the sub amounts for each category. Then figure out the final totals and record them in the appropriate spaces on Schedule C. Keep all your receipts in case the Internal Revenue Service calls on you to justify them.

Again, if you have just a few article sales, you would not have to record them on your income tax form. Check with a person knowledgeable about taxes on what amount of sales you would have to have for them to be recorded.

XI Photos Will Help To Sell Your Article

If you want to sell a travel article, photos will definitely help persuade the editor to buy your work. In fact, some editors will not accept the article unless you supply photos. Some editors purchase the text-photo package as one and do not offer any additional payment for photos, while others offer extra payment. Read the "Photographer's Guidelines" before submitting photos to the magazine. Sometimes the photographer's guidelines are separate or are incorporated in with the writer's guidelines. In either case, include a SASE (self-addressed, stamped envelope) when requesting the guidelines.

PHOTO TERMS

The following terms are ones that I think a travel writer should be familiar with:

Acetate – Transparent plastic film.

B & W – Abbreviation for black and white photograph. Editors usually prefer the 8x10 size.

Caption – Description of the subject matter of a photograph, including names of people where appropriate. Usually this information is placed under the photo. Also called a cutline.

Color separation – Separating the full-color transparency into the four basic color negatives for process printing.

Contrast — The tonal gradation between highlights and shadows.

Credit line — Giving proper credit if you have not taken the photo. The credit line is put after the caption and enclosed in parentheses.

Crop — Cutting a photo down so that it will fit the space. The publication will take care of this.

Glossy — A black and white photograph with a shiny surface as opposed to one with a non-shiny matte finish.

Halftone — A reproduction of a continuous tone illustration (photograph or artwork) with the image formed by camera-screened dots of various sizes.

Kodalith — High-contrast film generally used in printing.

Master print — The very best darkroom result in a black and white photograph as opposed to a working print without all the refinements.

Matte finish — Dull-coated paper without gloss; some black and white photos have this finish.

Model release — A paper signed by the subject of a photograph (or his guardian, if a juvenile) giving the photographer permission to use the photograph, editorially or for advertising purposes or for some specific purpose as stated.

Photo feature — A feature in which photographs are emphasized rather than the accompanying written material.

PMT — Stands for Photo Mechanical Process, a Kodak process.

Portfolio — Folder for carrying photographic or artwork samples.

PSA — Stands for Photographic Society of America.

Slides — Usually called transparencies by editors who want color photographs.

Stock photo — Often tourist attractions and tourist offices have a selection of photos in stock that are available to writers if they request them. Usually they will be sent to the writer for free, especially if he or she is preparing a travel article.

Transparencies — Positive color slides which have a picture or design that is visible when light shines through them. Editors usually prefer these sizes: 35 mm, 2¼x2¼ or larger.

POINTS TO CONSIDER WHEN TAKING PHOTOS
If you decide to take your own photos, here are several points to consider to make them better. In addition, you should read some photography books or attend a photography class.

- Try to have a single dominating or main point of interest. Do not overcrowd your picture with too many objects.

- Choose a background for a figure or group. This could be a doorway, clump of bushes, landscape or shoreline. This background will serve as a setting or frame for your photo.

- Equalize light and dark tones. For example, all of the dark values should not be in one place. Gradations from light to dark tones are needed.

- Let your subjects look natural, not like they are posing.

- If you are doing a series of photos, try to achieve

continuity.

- Try for an unusual viewpoint. Do not hold your camera level all the time, move it up or down. Then snap—you should get a unique result.

- Obtain a three-dimension effect through a variety of lighting. This will add depth to your photo. You do not always have to have light coming from behind your photos.

- Frame your architectural photos; this will make them less commonplace. For example, a castle could be framed by foliage and a fence.

- To achieve a soft "atmospheric" effect, rather than sharp detail, try diffusing some of your subjects.

- Here are a few tips for taking photos of flowers. Proper lighting is one of the foundations for good flower photos. Remember that shadows are necessary to reproduce form properly in any graphic illustration. As a general rule, bright, direct, overhead light is not desirable for flower photos. The best results are obtained in the earlier morning hours or toward the end of the day when the direction of light is from the side.

- If you are taking a photo of a moving figure or object, move your camera in unison with it. This will avoid blurring.

- If you are taking color photos, flat and even lighting is essential. Lighting one part of your subject much more strongly than the rest will make other parts much too dark and color will be lost. This applies to the principal subject, background and foreground.

OBTAINING PHOTOS
If you feel that you would not take good photos or do

not have the time, you can easily obtain photos from the tourist attraction you are writing the article about or from the state tourist office where the attraction is located. Also, the state chamber of commerce may have photos.

Here is a sample letter you can send to the tourist attraction. If you send it to the Public Information Officer, it should get to the right person.

Date

Public Information Officer
Address

Dear (name):

I am writing an article on the Henry Ford Museum and Greenfield Village in Dearborn, Michigan. I need photographs to accompany the article. Would you please send me some glossy black and white photos (8x10 size, preferably) of the automobiles and other attractions in the museum?

Also, I would appreciate updated information on the hours the sites are open, admission costs, special events scheduled for the next six months or year, and any other helpful information.

If the article is published, I will be happy to send you a copy. I hope to hear from you in the very near future.

Sincerely,

Name
Address

In my experience, by writing a letter like this, the public information officer would send an entire packet containing photos as well as information on dates and hours the site is open, admission costs and the schedule of special events. This information is very helpful because you may not have the time to write your article immediately and this way

71

you would have updated information.

You may not receive as high a payment for photos that you did not take. On the other hand, you may be paid the same amount as if you took your own photos. It depends on the editor.

WRITING CAPTIONS

In order to obtain an idea of how to write photo captions, look through magazines and newspapers. Captions contain few words. They should capture the attention of the reader.

Using the Henry Ford Museum photo with a family standing in front of it, here is what a caption might say: "This family is enjoying the Henry Ford Museum and adjoining Greenfield Village. The museum is known for its outstanding selection of Ford and other automobiles. It is located in Dearborn, Michigan. (Photo courtesy of Office of Public Relations, Greenfield Village and Henry Ford Museum, Dearborn, Michigan.)"

A number of methods can be used to type captions. For black and white photos, type the caption on a sheet of paper and tape it to the bottom of the back of the photo with masking tape. This will allow the editor to easily remove the copy for typesetting. The caption should fold over the front of the photo so that the editor can fold it back for easy reading. Another method is to type the captions on a separate sheet of paper and assign each a number corresponding with its photo. The paper can be placed before the packet of photos.

Captions for color transparencies, 2¼x2¼ size or larger, can be typed on thin strips of paper inserted in the acetate sleeve protecting the transparency. For 35 mm transparencies, type the captions on a separate sheet and assign corresponding numbers. Color prints are not acceptable in most cases.

Each black and white photograph should carry your name and address on the back and some identifying number (written lightly on the back of the photo in pencil, so as not to damage the photo surface itself).

For color transparencies—your name and address, and some picture identification can be placed on the small mounts; the rest can be typed on a separate sheet. The transparencies, each in a transparent protective sleeve, can be hinged with tape to the top of the caption sheet.

MODEL RELEASE

Most magazines and newspapers do not require releases on photographs to be used strictly for editorial illustrations. But a model release is required for all recognizable persons in a picture which is to be used for advertising purposes (including photographs appearing on a magazine cover, in sponsored publications, company brochures, etc.). The release is used, for example, if you actually appeared in the photo, or if someone else did. There is a possibility that you could be in one of your photos accompanying your travel article if someone else took your photo.

The release protects the photographer against possible suits for invasion of privacy or legal damages, since many states have laws which forbid a name, picture or quotation from being used for commercial purposes without the subject's authorization.

If the person in the photograph is a minor, the release must be signed by his or her parents or guardians.

Never send your original model release along with a photograph. Instead send a copy and keep the original in your files.

A sample model release could read this way:

In consideration for value received, receipt whereof is acknowledged, I (your name) hereby give (name of firm or publication) the absolute right and permission to copyright and/or publish, and/or re-sell photographic portraits or pictures of me, or in which I may be included in whole or in part, for art, advertising, trade or any other lawful purpose whatsoever.

I (your name) hereby waive any right that I may have to inspect and/or approve the finished product or the advertising copy that may be used in connection therewith, or the use to which it may be applied.

I (your name) release, discharge and agree to save (name of firm or publication) from any liability by virtue of any blurring, distortion, alteration, optical illusion or use in composite form, whether intentional or otherwise, that may occur or be produced in the making of said pictures, or in any processing tending towards the completion of the finished product.

Signature_____ Model_____

Date_____ Address_____

Witness_____ _____

PACKING PHOTOS
Here are some helpful hints for packing photos:

- If you typed your captions on a separate sheet(s), put this sheet first before the photographs.

- Pick up corrugated cardboard inserts from your local grocery store.

- Place your black and white photos between two corrugated cardboard inserts, wrap two rubber bands around them, and mail the photos with your manuscript in a 9x12 or 10x13 size envelope. If you have numerous photos, you may want to pack them separately from your manuscript.

- To mail transparencies, use slotted acetate sheets, which hold twenty slides and offer protection from scratches, moisture, dirt and dust. These acetate sheets are available in standard sizes from most photo supply houses. Do not use glass mounts. Mail the transparencies like you would black and white photos.

- Because transparencies are irreplaceable (unless you have negatives or duplicates made), be sure to insure them.

- Print "PHOTOS ENCLOSED - DO NOT BEND" on the outer mailing envelope.

- Enclosed a self-addressed, stamped envelope in case your materials would be returned. Be sure that postage is sufficient for both the photos and manuscript. You can attach the stamps to the inner envelope with a paper clip or in a separate small envelope. This way if your materials were not returned, the editor could send you back the postage. Usually, though, they keep it. One outer envelope and one inner envelope (folded — same size) are usually enough unless you have a large manuscript and numerous photos to mail.

XII Addresses Of State Tourist Offices

You may find the following addresses of state tourist offices very helpful, especially if you would like to obtain photos or up-dated information on various tourist attractions. This would be in addition to writing the specific tourist attraction. Just write to the appropriate office. All of the addresses were taken from a book titled, *State Administrative Officials Classified By Functions*. I omitted the names of the directors and telephone numbers because they may have changed.

The tourist offices are listed alphabetically by state.

ALABAMA
Bureau of Publicity and Information
Development Office
Room 403, Highway Building
Montgomery, Alabama 36130

ALASKA
Division of Tourism
Department of Commerce and Economic Development
Pouch E
Juneau, Alaska 99811

ARIZONA
Office of Tourism
Governor's Office of Economic Planning
  and Development
Room 501, West Wing
State Capitol
Phoenix, Arizona 85007

ARKANSAS
Tourism Division
Department of Parks and Tourism
No. 1, Capitol Mall
Little Rock, Arizona 72201

COLORADO
Division of Commerce and Development
Department of Local Affairs
Room 500, 1313 Sherman Street
Denver, Colorado 80203

CONNECTICUT
Department of Economic Development
210 Washington Street
Hartford, Connecticut 06115

DELAWARE
Division of Economic Development
Department of Community Affairs and Economic
  Development
630 State College Road
Dover, Delaware 19901

DISTRICT OF COLUMBIA
Office of Business and Economic Development
1350 E Street, NW
Washington, DC 20004

FLORIDA
Division of Tourism
Department of Commerce
107 Gaines Street
Collins Building
Tallahassee, Florida 32304

GEORGIA
Tourist Division
Department of Industry and Trade
1400 N. Omni International
Atlanta, Georgia 30303

HAWAII
Tourism Office
Department of Planning and Economic Development
P. O. Box 2359
Honolulu, Hawaii 96813

IDAHO
Division of Tourism and Industrial Development
Office of the Governor
Room 108, State House
Boise, Idaho 83720

ILLINOIS
Economic Development Services Division
Department of Commerce and Community Affairs
222 S. College
Springfield, Illinois 62706

INDIANA
Lieutenant Governor
State House
Indianapolis, Indiana 46204

IOWA
Travel Development Division
Travel Development Council
250 Jewett Building
Des Moines, Iowa 50319

KANSAS
Travel and Tourism Division
Economic Development Department
503 Kansas Avenue
Topeka, Kansas 66603

KENTUCKY
Business Development and Research Division
Department of Commerce
Frankfort, Kentucky 40601

Advertising Programs, Media Relations, Hospitality
Education
Department of Commerce
Fort Boone Plaza
Frankfort, Kentucky 40601

LOUISIANA
Office of Tourism and Promotion
Department of Culture, Recreation and Tourism
P. O. Box 44291
Baton Rouge, Louisiana 70804

MAINE
Development Office
Executive Department
State House
Augusta, Maine 04333

MARYLAND
Tourist Development
Division of Economic Development
Department of Economic and Community
 Development
1748 Forest Drive
Annapolis, Maryland 21401

MASSACHUSETTS
Division of Tourism
Department of Commerce and Development
Executive Office of Manpower Affairs
13th Floor, 100 Cambridge
Boston, Massachusetts 02202

MICHIGAN
Travel Bureau
Department of Commerce
Law Building
Lansing, Michigan 48909

MINNESOTA
Tourism Division
Department of Economic Development
Hanover Building
480 Cedar Street
St. Paul, Minnesota 55101

MISSISSIPPI
Tourism Development
Department of Agriculture and Commerce
P. O. Box 849
Jackson, Mississippi 39205

MISSOURI
Division of Tourism
Department of Consumer Affairs
308 E. High Street
Jefferson City, Missouri 65101

MONTANA
Travel Promotion Unit
Department of Highways
1236 Sixth Avenue
Helena, Montana 59601

NEBRASKA
Division of Travel and Tourism
Department of Economic Development
P. O. Box 94666
Lincoln, Nebraska 68509

NEVADA
Division of Travel and Tourism
Department of Economic Development
Heroes Memorial Building
108 W. Second Street
Carson City, Nevada 89710

NEW HAMPSHIRE
Office of Vacation Travel Promotion
Department of Resources and Economic Development
6 Loudon Road
Concord, New Hampshire 03301

NEW JERSEY
Division of Travel and Tourism
Department of Labor and Industry
Labor and Industry Building
John Fitch Plaza
Trenton, New Jersey 08625

NEW MEXICO
Tourism and Travel Division
Commerce and Industry Department
Bataan Memorial Building
Santa Fe, New Mexico 87503

NEW YORK
Division of Tourism
Department of Commerce
230 Park Avenue
New York City, New York 10017

NORTH CAROLINA
Division of Travel and Tourism Development
Department of Commerce
P. O. Box 25249
Raleigh, North Carolina 27611

NORTH DAKOTA
Travel Division
Highway Department
Highway Building, Capitol Grounds
Bismarck, North Dakota 58505

OHIO
Travel and Tourism Office
Department of Economic and Community
 Development
30 E. Broad Street
Columbus, Ohio 43215

OKLAHOMA
Tourism and Recreation Department
500 Will Rogers Memorial Office Building
State Capitol Complex
Oklahoma, Oklahoma 73105

OREGON
Travel Information Council
Room 501, Executive House
325 Thirteenth Street, NE
Salem, Oregon 97310

PENNSYLVANIA
Bureau of Travel Development
Department of Commerce
206 South Office Building
Harrisburg, Pennsylvania 17120

RHODE ISLAND
Tourism Division
Department of Economic Development
1 Weybosset Hill
Providence, Rhode Island 02903

SOUTH CAROLINA
Department of Parks, Recreation and Tourism
Edgar A. Brown Building
Columbia, South Carolina 29201

SOUTH DAKOTA
Department of Economic and Tourism Development
Foss Building
Pierre, South Dakota 57501

TENNESSEE
Department of Tourist Development
Fesslers Lane
Nashville, Tennessee 37210

TEXAS
Tourist Development Board
P. O. Box 12008
Capitol Station
Austin, Texas 78711

UTAH
Division of Travel Development
Office of Community and Economic Development
Council Hall
Salt Lake City, Utah 84114

VERMONT
Travel Division
Agency of Development and Community Affairs
60 Elm Street
Montpelier, Vermont 05602

VIRGINIA
Virginia State Travel Service
6 N. Sixth Street
Richmond, Virginia 23219

WASHINGTON
Travel Development Division
Department of Commerce and Economic
 Development
101 General Administration Building
Olympia, Washington 98504

WEST VIRGINIA
Travel Development Division
Governor's Office of Economic and Community
 Development
Room 553, Building 6
State Capitol Complex
Charleston, West Virginia 25305

WISCONSIN
Division of Tourism
Department of Business Development
123 W. Washington, No. 650
Madison, Wisconsin 53702

WYOMING
Travel Commission
Etchepare Circle
Cheyenne, Wyoming 82002

XIII   Addresses Of State Chambers Of Commerce

Besides contacting the state tourist offices, you may also want to contact the state chambers of commerce about a specific tourist attraction. They will provide you with updated information on admission rates, special events, etc., as well as photos. All of these will usually be sent for free. Check through the *World Wide Chamber of Commerce Directory* which comes out annually. It contains state and city chambers of commerce.

The following is a list of chambers of commerce listed alphabetically by state. Again, I have omitted the names of officers because they change.

ALABAMA
Alabama Chamber of Commerce
468 S. Perry Street
P. O. Box 76
Montgomery, Alabama 36101

ALASKA
Alaska State Chamber of Commerce
310 2nd Street
Juneau, Alaska 99801

ARIZONA
Arizona Chamber of Commerce
3216 N. 3rd Street, No. 103
Phoenix, Arizona 85012

ARKANSAS
Arkansas State Chamber of Commerce
911 Wallace Building
Little Rock, Arkansas 72201

CALIFORNIA
California Chamber of Commerce
455 Capitol Mall, Suite 300
P. O. Box 1736
Sacramento, California 95808

COLORADO
Colorado Association of Commerce and Industry
1390 Logan Street
Denver, Colorado 80203

CONNECTICUT
Connecticut Business and Industry Association
60 Washington Street
Hartford, Connecticut 06100

DELAWARE
Delaware State Chamber of Commerce
1102 West Street
Wilmington, Delaware 19801

DISTRICT OF COLUMBIA
Chamber of Commerce of the United States
1615 H Street, N.W.
Washington, D.C. 20062

FLORIDA
Florida State Chamber of Commerce
136 S. Bronough Street
P. O. Box 5497
Tallahassee, Florida 32301

GEORGIA
Georgia Chamber of Commerce
1200 Commerce Building
Atlanta, Georgia 30303

HAWAII
The Chamber of Commerce of Hawaii
735 Bishop Street
Honolulu, Hawaii 96813

IDAHO
Idaho Association of Commerce and Industry
414 Simplot Building
P. O. Box 389
Boise, Idaho 83701

ILLINOIS
Illinois State Chamber of Commerce
20 N. Wacker Drive
Chicago, Illinois 60606

INDIANA
Indiana State Chamber of Commerce
2nd Floor, Board of Trade Building
143 N. Meridian Street
Indianapolis, Indiana 46204

IOWA
Iowa Chamber of Commerce
Hotel Burlington
Burlington, Iowa 52601

KANSAS
Kansas Association of Commerce and Industry
500 First National Bank Tower
Topeka, Kansas 66603

KENTUCKY
Kentucky Chamber of Commerce
P. O. Box 817
Frankfort, Kentucky 40602

LOUISIANA
Louisiana Association of Business and Industry
Capitol House Hotel
Suite 200
P. O. Box 3988
Baton Rouge, Louisiana 70821

MAINE
Maine State Chamber of Commerce
One Canal Plaza
P. O. Box 65
Portland, Maine 04112

MARYLAND
Maryland Chamber of Commerce
60 West Street, Suite 405
Annapolis, Maryland 21401

MASSACHUSETTS
Massachusetts Chamber of Commerce
c/o Department of Commerce and Development
Leverett Saltonstall Building
Government Center
100 Cambridge Street
Boston, Massachusetts 02202

MICHIGAN
Michigan State Chamber of Commerce
Business and Trade Center
Suite 400
200 N. Washington Square
Lansing, Michigan 48933

MINNESOTA
Greater Minneapolis Chamber of Commerce
15 S. 5th Street
Minneapolis, Minnesota 55402

MISSISSIPPI
Mississippi Economic Council
656 Building
656 N. State
Jackson, Mississippi 39201

MISSOURI
Missouri State Chamber of Commerce
428 E. Capitol Avenue
P. O. Box 149
Jefferson City, Missouri 65102

MONTANA
Montana State Chamber of Commerce
110 Neill Avenue
P. O. Box 1730
Helena, Montana 59601

NEBRASKA
Nebraska Association of Commerce and Industry
424 Terminal Building
P. O. Box 81556
Lincoln, Nebraska 68501

NEVADA
Nevada State Chamber of Commerce
P. O. Box 2806
Reno, Nevada 89505

NEW HAMPSHIRE
Division of Economic Development
6 Park Street
P. O. Box 856
Concord, New Hampshire 03301

NEW JERSEY
New Jersey State Chamber of Commerce
5 Commerce Street
Newark, New Jersey 07102

NEW MEXICO
Greater Albuquerque Chamber of Commerce
401 Second Street, N.W.
Albuquerque, New Mexico 87102

NEW YORK
Empire State Chamber of Commerce
150 State Street
Albany, New York 12207

NORTH CAROLINA
Greater Winston-Salem Chamber of Commerce
P. O. Box 1408
Winston-Salem, North Carolina 27102

NORTH DAKOTA
Greater North Dakota Association
107 Roberts Street
P. O. Box 2467
Fargo, North Dakota 58102

OHIO
Ohio Chamber of Commerce
17 S. High Street
Columbus, Ohio 43215

OKLAHOMA
Oklahoma State Chamber of Commerce
4020 N. Lincoln
Oklahoma City, Oklahoma 73105

OREGON
Oregon Chamber of Commerce
824 S.W. 5th Avenue
Portland, Oregon 97204

PENNSYLVANIA
Pennsylvania Chamber of Commerce
222 N. 3rd Street
Harrisburg, Pennsylvania 17101

RHODE ISLAND
Greater Providence Chamber of Commerce
10 Dorrance Street
Providence, Rhode Island 02903

SOUTH CAROLINA
South Carolina Chamber of Commerce
1002 Calhoun Street
Columbia, South Carolina 29201

SOUTH DAKOTA
South Dakota Chamber of Commerce
222 E. Capitol
P. O. Box 190
Pierre, South Dakota 57501

TENNESSEE
Tennessee Chamber of Commerce
161 4th Avenue, North
Nashville, Tennessee 37219

TEXAS
Texas State Chamber of Commerce
815 Brazos
Austin, Texas 78701

UTAH
Utah Chamber of Commerce
19 E. 2nd Street
Salt Lake City, Utah 84111

VERMONT
Vermont State Chamber of Commerce
P. O. Box 37
Montpelier, Vermont 05602

VIRGINIA
Virginia State Chamber of Commerce
611 E. Franklin Street
Richmond, Virginia 23219

WASHINGTON
Washington Chamber of Commerce
W. 1020 Riverside Avenue
P. O. Box 2147
Spokane, Washington 99210

WEST VIRGINIA
West Virginia Chamber of Commerce
1101 Kanawha Valley Building
P. O. Box 2789
Charleston, West Virginia 25330

WISCONSIN
Wisconsin Association of Manufacturers and Commerce
111 E. Wisconsin Avenue
Suite 1600
Milwaukee, Wisconsin 53202

WYOMING
Wyoming Chamber of Commerce
399 Bridger Avenue
P. O. Box 398
Rock Springs, Wyoming 82901

XIV Teaching A Travel Writing Workshop/Class

If you enjoy selling your travel articles and would like to share with others how you do it, you should consider teaching a travel writing workshop or class. It is still another way to add to your writing income.

Late in 1980, I had the idea of teaching a writing class. I suggested the idea to the Director of the Writing Program for Adults, Division of Urban Outreach, University of Wisconsin—Milwaukee and Extension. I work at the university. She was interested in the fact that I wrote travel articles and asked me to work up a plan of what I would cover in three sessions dealing with travel writing.

The workshop would be especially for writers, travel agents, students or anyone who would like to learn more about travel writing and how to market their works. Here is how my plan looked.

Session 1: Travel Writing Markets — Publications that were currently buying travel articles as well as how to gear an article to a specific market were discussed. Elements of a good travel article were elaborated on with examples of the instructor's work used to illustrate these points.

Session 2: Taking A Trip — In this session, the class and instructor took a three hour trip to the Milwaukee Public Museum. It was a self-guided tour. Workshop participants were asked to take notes and write an article about their trip to the museum. Participants were free to use any approach they wanted to in developing the article but the length was to be about 500 words.

Session 3: Critiquing Articles — The instructor and workshop participants did a general critique on the articles written about the museum visit. Each participant was asked to read his or her article to the class. If the participants wanted a more detailed critique, they were asked to leave their articles with the instructor. They were also asked to provide a stamped, self-addressed envelope so their work could be returned through the mail. There was not enough time to do a detailed critique in class because of the time and number of participants. Each session was from 2 to 3 hours.

I am happy to say that the workshop was a success the first time it was held in 1981. It attracted about 15 people, just the perfect size for such a workshop. I think the fact that the workshop was held on three consecutive Saturday mornings was one reason why it was popular. Quite a few people commented that they enjoyed coming on a Saturday rather than an evening after a day of work. Also, the workshop was offered for $45.00, which was a reasonable fee. Participants did not work for a grade but earned continuing education units.

Because the workshop was a success in 1981, it was offered again in 1982.

PUBLICITY HELPS

I think another reason why the workshop was a success was that it was publicized in various ways. The Director of the Writing Program for Adults took care of most of the publicity. First, a general brochure was written up and distributed to people who had previously participated in the Writing Program for Adults. It was also distributed to travel agents.

In 1981, a brochure was done on the travel writing workshop alone. Because of less money in the 1982 budget, my travel writing workshop was included with other writing classes, all in the same brochure.

Other ways in which my travel writing workshop was promoted was a small display ad in The Milwaukee Journal (local daily newspaper - travel section) and through radio spots (university radio).

Lastly, I wrote some news releases on the workshop. I enjoy promoting my workshops. These releases were sent to the travel editor of The Milwaukee Journal and The Milwaukee Sentinel (both local daily newspapers), to Community Newspapers (a chain of 21 weekly newspapers in Milwaukee and the suburbs), to the South Side Spirit (a local weekly newspaper), the University of Wisconsin-Milwaukee campus newspaper, and to the University of Wisconsin-Milwaukee faculty/staff newsletter. The same release was sent to all the publications. I feel that these news releases are valuable because they are free publicity except for postage and typing paper. I also feel that they are effective ways to promote a travel writing workshop/class.

THE NEWS RELEASE

As I said earlier, I composed a news release which was sent to the publications described in the above paragraph. It told where, when and what the workshop would deal with. The news release should be typed on white paper and double spaced. It should be sent out to the various editors about one month ahead of the starting date. Here is how my release read for the 1982 workshop (the second year for the workshop):

FROM THE DESK OF RUTH WUCHERER
TELEPHONE NUMBER
DATE
FOR IMMEDIATE RELEASE

TRAVEL WRITING WORKSHOP
TO BE OFFERED

A 3-session workshop on travel writing is being offered through the Writing Program for Adults, Division of Urban Outreach, University of Wisconsin-Milwaukee and Extension. The workshop, which will start on October 16, 1982 [made up date, my workshop was earlier] will be taught by Ruth Wucherer, a local freelance writer.

The workshop is especially for writers, travel agents, students, or anyone who would like to learn more about travel writing and how to market their works. The instructor has a number of freelance writing credits to her name, including travel articles.

The first session will deal with travel article markets and writing techniques. A trip to the Experimental Aircraft Association Museum is planned for the second session. Workshop participants will be asked to write an article about their visit to the museum and these articles will be critiqued by the instructor and class in the third session.

The fee for the workshop is $40.00, plus $2.25 for the museum admission. For further information, please call the Writing Program for Adults at (telephone number).

COVER LETTER

When you send the news releases to the newspaper, a cover letter should accompany it. It should explain why you are sending the news release. Single space it. A sample of what the cover letter should say is on page 101.

I type each news release and cover letter individually, rather than xerox it. I think this is more professional and your material is more likely to be read by editors. Besides there are not that many news releases and cover letters to type. You use the same ones throughout.

Just a word on seeing the published version of your news release. . .do not be discouraged if it was cut because of space limitations. This is often the case, although I have found that local weekly newspapers will usually use all of the material. Also, xerox additional copies of the published version if it appears in the newspaper or other publications. Keep them in your files. You may need them in the future.

```
                                          Date

     Name of Editor
     Publication
     Address

     Dear (name of editor):
        Enclosed find a news release on an upcoming
     Travel Writing Workshop that I will be teaching.
     I will appreciate it if you can publish this infor-
     mation in one of your upcoming issues. If you
     have any questions, please contact me.

                          Cordially,
                          (Name, address,
                          telephone number)

        Enclosure (include brochure if you have one)
```

TRAVEL WRITING CLASS

If your travel writing workshop is a success, you might think of teaching a travel writing class. It could be modeled after the workshop but cover a longer period of time. I am trying to sell this idea to local junior colleges in the Milwaukee area and the university where I work.

XV Reference Materials For Travel Article Writers

Here are a list of reference books that may help you in writing your travel articles. This is just a sampling; there are many more. Most are probably available from your local library. A few can be obtained for a small fee from your local bookstore.

HOTEL & MOTEL RED BOOK

Hotel & Motel Red Book. This book lists hotels, motels and resorts in the United States and other countries. It is the official directory of the American Hotel and Motel Association and is issued annually by the American Hotel Association Directory Corporation, 888 Seventh Avenue, New York, New York 10019. The address, telephone number, owner and/or manager's name, and what credit cards the establishment accepts are given.

AMERICAN YOUTH HOSTELS HANDBOOK

American Youth Hostels Handbook. If you like to travel frequently and do not have much money, you may consider staying at a hostel which is a low cost, supervised, overnight accommodation for people traveling for health, education and recreation. This handbook grades (from "shelter" to "superior") hostels throughout the United States. It also gives helpful information; such as, cost for staying at the hostel, when it is open, what sports are available at the site or nearby, etc.

The word "youth" is somewhat misleading in the title because all ages are welcome at the United States hostels. However, due to local ordinance, a few hostels cannot accept individual hostelers under the age of 18 without parental permission.

The handbook is published annually by American Youth Hostels, Inc., National Administrative Offices, 1332 I Street Northwest — 8th Floor, Washington, D.C. 20005.

VISITOR ACCOMMODATIONS FACILITIES AND SERVICES

Visitor Accommodations Facilities and Services. This booklet lists alphabetically by areas the overnight accommodations and other facilities and services concessioners provide for travelers in the National Park System. For example, some of the parks covered include Glacier National Park, Grand Canyon National Park, Yellowstone National Park and Yosemite National Park.

The booklet is put out by the Department of the Interior and can be purchased from the Superintendent of Documents, U. S. Government Printing Office, Washington, D.C. 20402.

RAND MC NALLY ATLASES

Atlases. Rand McNally, a publisher, puts out a variety of atlases. For example, if you had to provide a map with your article, you could use these atlases as a guide. You could not copy them, though, unless you obtained special permission to do so.

Rand McNally & Company offices are located at: P.O. Box 7600, Chicago, Illinois 60680; 10 East 53rd Street, New York, New York 10022; and 595 Market Street, Suite 2130, San Francisco, California 94105.

NATIONAL PARK GUIDE

National Park Guide. This guide, which features all 48 national parks in the United States, is published by Rand McNally. Besides the special attractions of each park, a history is also given. A helpful reference guide if you are writing about your traveling experience in a national park.

FODOR'S TRAVEL GUIDES
Fodor's Travel Guides. Fodor publishes guides: area guides, country guides, U.S.A. regional guides, city guides, U.S.A. special interest guides and special interest guides (international). Averages 70 titles a year.

For example, *Fodor's Midwest 1979* covers the states of Illinois, Indiana, Iowa, Michigan, Minnesota, Ohio and Wisconsin. For each state, the following is listed: hotels and motels, restaurants and special attractions.

If you are a writer and have extensive knowledge of an area, you might want to submit your name to Fodor's Travel Guides, 2 Park Avenue, New York, New York 10016. They hire writers and/or experts for a fee, according to the *1984 Writer's Market*. Does not solicit manuscripts on a royalty basis.

MUSEUMS OF THE WORLD
Museums of the World (3rd Revised Edition). This book lists world museums, including those in the United States.

The specialty of each museum is given. Examples include the Scalamandre Museum of Textiles in New York; the Arizona Mineral Museum in Phoenix; and The Presidential Museum in Odessa, Texas. The book is published by K. G. Sauer Verlag KG, Munchen.

TRAVELORE REPORT
Travelore Report is a monthly newsletter for affluent travelers: businessmen, retirees, well-educated. It publishes material on specific tips, tours and bargain opportunities in travel. Brief insights of 25 to 200 words with facts, prices, names of hotels and restaurants, etc., on offbeat subjects of interest to people going places are needed.

Travel writers can submit items to this publication or subscribe to it themselves for a handy reference. The address is: Travelore Report, 225 S. 15th Street, Philadelphia,

Pennsylvania 19102.

LOCAL TRAVEL AGENCIES
Your *local travel agencies* have a variety of brochures on trips, cruises, etc., in the United States and abroad. You probably can obtain this information for free.

WEBSTER.S DICTIONARY
Every travel writer should keep *Webster's Dictionary* at his or her side. The dictionary not only gives correct spellings, but also contains a guide to punctuation and what form should be used for manuscripts.

I use *Webster's New World Dictionary of the American Language* but all Webster dictionaries are good.

THE BEST FREE ATTRACTIONS
The Best Free Attractions. Meadowbrook Press — 18318 Minnetonka Boulevard, Deephaven, Minnesota 55391 — puts out four books (by John Whitman) on attractions in the midwestern, southern, western and eastern United States. Each book contains 1,500 things to do and see for free. These include: sports events, films, scenic drives and historic sites. Each book costs $3.95, plus tax, and can be obtained from your local bookstore.

FREE STUFF FOR TRAVELERS
Free Stuff for Travelers is a paperback book also published by Meadowbrook Press. It contains information on 1,000 free things travelers can obtain by just writing for them--travel guides from all 50 states and 17 foreign countries, maps, newsletters, posters, lodging directories and more. The book costs $2.95, plus tax, and can be obtained from your local bookstore.

About The Author

Ruth Wucherer is an avid traveler. She has written numerous travel articles which have been published in a variety of publications. She has taught writing and travel writing classes.

Besides her published travel writings, she has had feature and business articles published. Her longer, published works include one book, *How To Sell Your Crafts*, and three booklets — *The Fascinating World of Advertising*, *What You Should Know About Credit* and *Make Money Selling Your Crafts*.

She resides in Milwaukee, Wisconsin.